THE

NARROWS

Also by Daniel Tobin

poetry

Where the World is Made (1999)

Double Life (2004)

prose

Passage to the Center: Imagination and the Sacred
in the Poetry of Seamus Heaney (1999)

THE
NARROWS

poems by **DANIEL TOBIN**

Four Way Books
New York City

Distributed by
University Press of New England
Hanover and London

Editorial Office
Four Way Books
POB 535, Village Station
New York, NY 10014
www.fourwaybooks.com

Library of Congress Catalogue Card Number: 2004101054

ISBN: 1-884800-59-9

Cover design by Pablo A. Medina for Cubanica

 Publication of this book is made possible in part by
an award from the National Endowment for the Arts,
which believes that a great nation deserves great art,
and by a generous grant from a private foundation.

NATIONAL
ENDOWMENT
FOR THE ARTS

This book is manufactured in the United States of America and
printed on acid-free paper.

Four Way Books is a not-for-profit organization. We are grateful
for the assistance we receive from individual donors, foundations,
and government arts agencies.

Distributed by University Press of New England
One Court Street, Lebanon, NH 03766

ACKNOWLEDGMENTS

The Alembic: "Long Jump Pit"
American Scholar: "Galilee"
Black Warrior Review: "Banshee"
Boulevard: "A Dolmen in the Burren," "Inishboffin Suite,"
    "Near Hag's Head," "Twentieth Century Limited"
Cape Rock: "Skytop," "Barkaloo Cemetery"
Chariton Review: "The Avenue," "St. Anselm's," "The Apartments"
Comstock Review: "The Rings"
Crab Orchard Review: "Elegy," "The Rainbow Café"
The Cresset: "At the Tree of Many, One"
Cumberland Poetry Review: " A Coat," "Crossings," "The Mirror,"
    "My Mother at the House of Her Father's Fathers," "The Ring"
Dalhousie Review: "The Lift"
Florida Review: "Prelude: The Narrows"
Great River Review: "The Pier"
Greensboro Review: "Back Window," "Double-Life," "Wreck"
Image: "Aftermath"
Literary Imagination: "Two Blackouts"
The Malahat Review: "Tattoo"
The Marlboro Review: "The Other Half"
Meridian: "Prospect"
Natural Bridge: "My Grandmother's Apartment," "St. John"
New Hibernia: "The Narrows"
Nua: "At the Lower East Side Tenement Museum"
Ploughshares: "Eye-Full Tower"
Poet Lore: "Stickball," "Blackout"
Poetry Ireland Review: "Ballsbridge, Dark Night"
Prism International: "According to Legend"
The Recorder: "Thinking of Meade Mountain,"
    "In the Green-wood," "Inheritors"
The Sewanee Review: "A Chalk Primavera on Eden Quay,"
    "The Dock Road"
Shenandoah: "A Mosque in Brooklyn," "Pallbearers at Emily
    Dickinson's Funeral"
Southern Humanities Review: "A Life Not Lived"
The Southern Review: "A Cemetery in Brooklyn"
Sou'wester: "Outerbridge Crossing"
Stand (England): "Thinking of Meade Mountain"
Tampa Review: "Broadcast," "Scar"
The Texas Review: "Drinking with My Father at Muse's Bar"
The Valparaiso Review: "Hope Chest," "The House"
The Virginia Quarterly Review: "My Mother's Eye"
Witness: "The Island"

"Bridge View" appeared in *Never Before: Poems About First Experiences* (New York: Four Way Books, 2005).

"Double-Life" received *The Greensboro Review* Poetry Prize.

"My Mother at the House of Her Father's Fathers" received the Donn Goodwin International Poetry Award.

"The Ring" is forthcoming in *Works of Mercy*, an anthology of poems about the Great Famine in Ireland, and received the Robert Penn Warren Poetry Prize.

I would also like to thank Ruth Anderson Barnett, Bruce Beasley, Christine Casson, Greg Delanty, Joy Manesiotis, Martha Rhodes, William Thompson, and William Wenthe for their invaluable advice and suggestions for organizing this sequence, and for their help revising some of these poems.

TABLE OF CONTENTS

This book is dedicated to Gerard Tobin
and Helen Tobin, in memoriam,
and to Christine Casson

The metaphysical desire does not long to return, for it is desire for a land not of our birth, for a land foreign to every nature which has not been the land of our parents, and to which we shall never betake ourselves.
               Emanuel Levinas

And Mael Duin said: "Leave the boat in rest without rowing and wherever it shall please God to bring, he will bring it." Then they entered the great, limitless ocean....
               "The Voyage of Mael Duin"

The brig St. John, from Galway, Ireland, laden with emigrants, was wrecked on Sunday morning.... Why care for these dead bodies? They really have no friends but the worms or fishes. Their owners were coming to the New World, as Columbus and the Pilgrims did,—they were within a mile of its shores; but, before they could reach it, they emigrated to a newer world than ever Columbus dreamed of... not merely mariner's tales and some paltry driftwood and sea-weed, but a continual drift and instinct to all our shores. I saw their empty hulks that came to land; but they themselves, meanwhile, were cast upon some shore yet further west, toward which we are all tending....
               Henry David Thoreau, "The Shipwreck"

PROEM: DOUBLE LIFE

The Sky Road

To have been born on the very edge of things
in a whitewashed hut with blonde bangs of thatch
and an unlatched gate that leads into the open,
sky and sky beyond the window onto land's end,
everything blending and the ocean shattered with light

and not to be this strange face peering through a hedge
your dead once walked beside, earrings of fuchsia
astride the rock wall: it is no nostalgia,
but the plain air of things, the very curb of exile,
this dwelling on the edge where you are born.

Headlands

To have driven along blue levitating roads
this far into land's end, golden, rumpled,
these humps that could be the goddess's bedclothes,
and that red brooch of a bridge pinning the continent
together; it is all ample and errant

like this wind and the garrulous ocean below
bellowing on in the voice of Whitman
Death, Death, Death, Death, Death on the wrong shore,
the horizon as much behind us as before,
always our eyes rising to the sky's imprint on tar.

I

THE NARROWS

THE NARROWS

The similitudes of the past and those of the future....

(for Nora Ruane, ni Hughes)

    I. Mural

The way Lanning painted it, Benton, Rivera—bright panels
on which the laborers huddle, shirtless, their flexed arms
bearing the full weight of the rail.
                       Representative men,
without names but for Paddy, Dago, Gook,
so the foreman calls them, shotgun slung behind his back
as he rides towards the Iron Horse somewhere deep
in the continent:
                   Death Valley and Donner Pass,
rock-faces sheer, indifferent—
        or patient, as if to say, *This rabble won't last long.*

To the left: natives lounge on empty prairie, wagons,
homesteaders tying bales of hay,
a horse-drawn thresher.
                To the right: turbines
squat as bombs, stokers at a furnace, a mother and infant
climbing into their crowded cart that will disappear
down the cavern walls of the street. A woman
leans out her window in a posture of regret.
          Someone leaving, someone not coming back,
while dead center of the mural others hammer the ties:

Lives scaled out of lives along the panorama's strict expanse....

     ℬ

My father drives the gaudy pink Rambler
down Bay Ridge Avenue to the Shore,

7

the great wooden pier jutting into the Narrows—flood-tide,
bright flow—where the ferry luffs against its moorings,
its wide iron ramp laid down for the line of cars that slow,
then roll snugly into its belly:
                              me in back between my mother
and her mother, Nora, who carries herself regally
as the Guggenheims whose children she nannied
when she first came over.
                              Quayside at Cobh,
under St. Colman's spire, she waited at the pier,
black Mayo dirt smoored into her shoes,
daughter of a remnant, of *clachan* and *rundale*,
cottier and *meithall*, the big ships made imaginable
on postcards distributed at crossroads in the townlands,
on signs posted in market villages: Dominion,
Cunard, White Star Line—"Splendid Accommodation"
for the exile, for the *deori*:
                              "There's nothing for you here."

        ℘

The tender putters to its floating palace,
in the distance, Spike Island, Davitt's Rock.
For days in steerage she's one of the thousand
packed inside, the bunks camp-hung and numbered,
the boat heaving
                    to the Atlantic, as though each roll
were prelude to an undertow.
It's nearly a week before she comes to the rail,
the ship steaming past Sandy Hook, the Moriches,
the Narrows a *causey* "of a highway where sky
comes down to water." There the Statue stands,
torch in hand
                    above the dumbstruck hordes,
above the gleaming cityscape, *caislean oir*,
castles of gold, mythic as Tir na nOg.

8

                    She's alone
as she queues off the gangway for the Great Hall
with its iron bars, an assembly line
of stations and pens, its marble alive with tongues.

It is as if the *throughother* of her familiar fields
had changed in a dream to which she now awakens,
the manifest tag pinned to her lapel,
a gripped inspection card, barked commands
from the uniform at the gate, from the uniform on the stairs.
She stiffens as she's handled, so many hands, her eyelids
twisted back with a buttonhook, the man ahead marked
with chalk, a brusque X on his coat
                        before he's shuffled away.
What's your name? Where are you going? What's your trade?
Have you a job? Can you read this?

    —"Let my sentence come forth from thy presence;
    let thine eyes behold the things that are equal."—

Then the shower, a baptism, the old world washed free.

                    And she's through,
the Island behind her with its dormitories and detainees,
caged yard and infirmary, walls glyphic with names,
the ferry bearing her to open road—fifty years:
a husband, five children, a first son outlived....

        ✍

Her Brooklyn of ample hills rises behind us,
bricked-up, paved over
as our ferry pushes into the Narrows
for our trip west. Ahead: Todt Hill, the terminal
at St. George. Skyscrapers crowd to the brink

of the Battery.
                    And as the boat loafs into the harbor—
                              a panorama of docks,
liners lumbering out to sea, tugs and tankers
where the bare steel towers of the bridge soar, half-risen,
over Gravesend,
          the Hudson pouring itself along the Palisades,
the Statue a green flame in the middle of it all.
                                    And already
my grandmother is out of the car for a better view,
shoring her new hat against the wind.

        II. Archive

How often have I dreamt this station's bare-bulbed dusk,
a distant clatter of wheels, the visible tremor
                              up the platform's spine
where pipe-water leaks along cracks of cement?
I look down the tunnel, watch the subway's double star
widen inside the passage, the din growing louder,
my back braced against a pillar as light
fans like a slow motion explosion along the ancient tiles
before the train bursts through, a cargo of bright rooms
riding the polished rails, filling the emptiness
of the ribbed archway:
                    The R Local at 86th and Fourth,
where I'd wait with my mother those few afternoons
we'd venture to the city.
                    Stay close, she'd tell me, don't go
by the tracks, watch for strangers. I'd keep near,
hold my ears against the screech.

        ∅

    10

The rules are strict inside the archive—no food, no bags,
no talking beyond this point.
                                    And don't forget
to take a number, line up for instruction
from the stern administrator, who, it turns out,
is politer than he looks, directing me patiently
in how to use the volumes of categories and codes,
as if these tomes were history's phone books,
as if each of us could dial our origins.

Registries, ships' lists, census reports, the boxes
            and their corresponding dates
piled ceiling high along the aisles
in the light's fluorescent haze.
            The archive is a Chinese box, a maze
that draws me further in, each filmed list
a laboratory slide of DNA—
                        Nora Ruane, ni Hughes,
of Kilvendoney. Her stone in Calvary
reads 1900, though she lied about her age, recited
the rosary in her small kitchen afternoons
when I came home from school,

      —"Get me a cruller, Danny, from Sally's,
      and yourself a hamburger and I'll make some tea..."—

For as long as I knew her she lived apart
from my grandfather, Martin, immobile
in a nursing home, our visits
become flickers in an unlit room.
Though my mother kept his passport—
British Subject, 1918, aged twenty years—
in the hope chest with her keepsakes.

In a gray, dated box I find the likely reels.
                                    Whir of machines

in the viewing room, the tape unspooling its microscopic lists,
bright squares like the subway's lit-up windows
across the black bar of film.
                          The cards, hastily typed,
run in spate down the screen where I sit, scanning the sounds
of names, until, finally, I read Martin Ruane,
arrived April 8th, 1920,
                          S.S. Kaiserin Auguste Victoria.
But how did he travel from Ballyhaunis
to Liverpool, the Prince's Dock, where the Irish were thick,
as Hawthorne wrote, "like maggots in cheese?"

                          And where did they meet, born
twenty miles apart, in different townlands?
            Not in the port, not in Claremorris.
For her name I need to scroll further back—
                          Harlan, Hellas, Hugo, Hughes:
ten Nora Hughes's—earliest 1910, most likely 1915—
arrived on *The Celtic* to New York out of Cobh.

Did they love each other?

            I'd heard of marriages arranged, families
gathered by county in their new neighborhoods.
In the photo she kept on her bedroom dresser
they looked so properly posed.

I remember how she grieved when he died,
keening her first son's name with her husband's
in the funeral parlor's smoky hall.

        ✐

Let's say I can see them
in the old apartment on Sixth.
In the dim light of that kitchen

Nora peels potatoes on newspaper;
Martin, a motorman, home from the subway,
turns on the radio while the baby
sleeps in his crib;
                    at the table, three daughters,
a first son just back from play
who will die within a week.

    —"I'll never get over it," my mother tells me
    years later, a seine of smoke drifting
    through the room, lit by a whiskey glass.—

Or let's say it's long after the war, the whole family
moved to Pearl Court. The sisters play cards
as the stereo hums The McNulty Family,
The Clancy Brothers:
                    Kitsch *clachan* in a beehive of brick.

Whiskey. Quarrels. Penny-ante.
Voices mingled in smoky fluorescence.
Nora in her housedress nursing
a shot and cigarette, dusk
fading through the slit blinds.

And let's say she predicts her own death, foreseen
        in a dream, the way as a girl she saw
        that man in his brown suit wandering
the fields of Kilvendoney
                who had died the day before....

        ✄

All the way back on the train
                        I watch the faces
of those around me. What do I have
but this clumsy reel of memory, this world

13

whirring past that fumbles away,
though I long to scroll it back,
                        to thread the spool
into the jumbled record of who I am?

I bring my trace home, even now
splicing the narrative together, sounding it out,
pasts made present already the past.

        III. West

To begin, love: our fingers on the map's crimped horizon,
following roads that run inland from the sea,
tracing the way west
                        in the clear light of our rented room—
Lucan, Clonard, Horseleap, Athlone, the names
reeling off,
                        lyrics sung to their own accompaniment,
all the way to Ballinrobe.
                                Outside, the teeming puzzle
of Dublin streets converges at the Liffey,
then out along the quays toward Kilmainham, Chapelizod.

                        It's all out of scale,
this naming and the thing named, as though the map
were territory,
                        and yet such frisson brings lift-off,
like the giddiness of our flight
above the Narrows, the city receding behind us, the bridge
grown small as a safety pin, clipping the islands
as we banked along the coast, leaving
the continent behind,
                        only a few boats below,

14

fish glistening into the ocean's huge nothing.

⌀

Who cares if it's all fiction, this romance of origins,
a farmhouse in a townland outside Ballinrobe,
stories rehearsed a hundred times
                              across a kitchen table?
How my grandmother had to leave, like her sisters
but one, Winnie, the youngest, turned back from Ellis Island,
a chalk "E" scratched on her coat, her eyes
already glazing under the buttonhook
into those two moons, and her stooped
as though searching for something lost.

Or how Tommy, her brother, ruled the house,
and would not let her visit family in America—
dollar bills pinned on walls beside holy pictures,
a brother and sister, like an old couple,
bent in silence before the hearth.

⌀

Here, driving free of town, the rotaries
run clockwise, the roadway
a mirror image of our familiar path.

My grandfather might have traveled east
along a version of this route
to one of the channel boats moored along the Liffey.
"Scholar," his passport read.
                    Did he leave for the "better life,"
like the millions who left because they had to go?

From Brize to Ballyhaunis, all the way to Eden Quay,
he followed the path of the long meadow,

as though to join that earlier train,
those who starved in their sod hovels,
                                        the sod itself
a last meal caking in their mouths.

And there was my grandfather, Martin, like Nora,
leaving by cart or train—who knows how?—
a generation later, finding their place
                                in the prospect
of a canvas too vast to envision whole.

                ∅

Is that what it means to be an American,
discovering yourself in the distances?—
                        Like a man on a Greyhound
that leaves the New York Port Authority
and takes the Lincoln Tunnel to the interstate.
It's after dark, all the man can see are headlights
                passing, a blur of malls and subdivisions.
He sleeps in his seat beside a stranger,
                        wakes when the bus pulls in
to a late-night road stop. He's not hungry,
but feels in his gut a tremor
                        of loneliness
that grows as they pass through Ohio, Indiana,
the furnaces of Hammond and Gary,
                fierce as Blake's Satanic mills,
spewing into the boundless prairie sky.
He looks out for a thousand miles
at the hypnotic emptiness of wheat fields and cornfields,
                the cinematic grandeur of the Rockies,
and descends from the Wasatch
                        to the Great Salt Lake,
sunset spreading over the earth....

16

What he wants
is to stand at the other end of it all, to see
the Pacific rolling into headlands
like visible waves of light,

                           and then to turn back,
the bridge stretching out over the bay below him,
another Narrows,

                 until he sees that there is no end,
just these waves of water waves of land
flung together,

                feeling on his face the rush of wind,
and inside him the growing thought that anywhere
might be home,

                 since home has become nowhere.

        ♋

It is like our standing present now
before this ancestral house

                        passed to unfamiliar hands,
its thatch removed years ago, a modern extension
jutting out back from whitewashed clay walls.

                        No one home.
And as we peer through the window,

                        the hearth inscribes its arc
halfway up the wall, its border painted brightly,
     an old-time kettle at the center—

                   Winnie dead, Tommy dead,
a line of unknown faces trailing back,

                        fanning forward,
our own to be among them,
as if now were the space between facing mirrors,
life's after-life of lives indwelling.

And already it's renewing itself,
the memory of our car ride across a country

                        that is not our own,
checking the map, stopping to find our bearings,
our lunch in a town called Gortaleam,
how we bickered about the right road,
but made our way—
                the church at the crossroads
in Robeen, the cemetery in the field
        where Winnie and Tommy are buried
with their parents, Sabena and Martin,
all the names on a single stone—
                        then, so close,
losing our way again, stopping to ask directions
to Kilvendoney—its four farmhouses on stony ground
twenty miles from the Atlantic,
        how the old farmer leaned his windblown face
to our window before pointing us the way:

        —"Is it Hughes you're wanting?
        Oh, they're all gone."

II

FROM THE COUNTRY
OF THE DEAD

THE PIER

You are your father's father
and the stream....

I.

That wild-man soaring out over the Narrows
from the half-painted bridge,
his length of rope an umbilical cord,
is my crazy Uncle Alan, family scop, teller of tall tales.

It was the days before his stroke, and my father
has driven our family the forty miles
from our house to the Jersey Shore to see
his older brother, the one born closest to him,
the raconteur of Cliffwood Beach
whom he looked on with pride.

In the story my uncle told that day
as we sat under the glow of patio lanterns,
the bridge tower rose above him, sheer as a butte,
while he lowered himself, ratcheting the rope
down its side, the steel uncoated, opaque,
then gleaming the blue-gray of a battleship
where he wielded his deft brush.

I still don't know if it was true.
It's become a family legend,
how he hung suspended on his own life-line,
tug after tug puttering below,
the cargo boats, battered garbage scows,
bound for Red Hook or the Kill Van Kull,
and among them now and then a liner
steaming regally into the harbor,
or out along the channel
that widens into the Atlantic.

II.

My father loved that story, I could tell
by his eyes, the satisfaction in his folded arms,
while twilight fell in a bloom of citronella
that made each face appear nearly rapt
as my own,
                    like whenever my father
unscrolled the paintings of the great ships
—*America, The United States*—that he'd kept
in the space behind his dresser.
Why hadn't he framed them, hung them
 in the living room in place of the mirror
that took up what seemed the entire wall?

The boats were nearly twins, sleek bulkheads,
stacks rising red, white, blue over decks
and staterooms, though *The United States*
looked sleeker still, its stacks angled back
with wings, only the faintest stroke of foam
where the prow parted the waves.

III.

What I could almost see those times
my father lifted them from their places
were the living passengers whirling
on the dance floor of a great ballroom,
and deeper down, under decks, the steerage
crowd playing cards or telling stories
in an amber glare of light on cast iron.

22

Now, further back, I can see shuttered
on the famine ship that brought them
here, my father's fathers, the tune
of a tin whistle ghosting the hold,
the whistler's fingers reeling over
its zeros while the dying shiver
each alone in a dance of fever.

St. John: stench of lazar house,
stunned hush of a remnant as bodies
pile behind, or drift, picked clean,
under waves. And ahead, the work—
someone singing through the smoke-haze
and clatter of a bar, someone spinning
a story out over the abyss again.

IV.

My father on the patio of his brother's house
thirty years ago, youngest of ten, swaddles
in his usual deferral—"Al, you tell the story,"
as the conversation turns to Red Hook,
their growing up, tales of a drunk father,
of a good mother who served: the tired
repetitions, the ancient history, floating
like spindrift into shallows, recurrent dream
that flexes my father's hands, his desire to speak
broken by the fear of being outdone.

Years later, both drunk, I sit with him alone,
a hint of dawn catching the blinds:
"No one wanted me after my mother died,
none of my brothers." And he says a name,

"John Harvey," the heel of his hand pressed
tightly to his forehead. "I was stationed
in the Navy Yard. We were playing
in the barracks with our new guns."
His rhythm shudders. "I shot him.
We were only goddamn seventeen."

My father plants his fist deeper
into the space above his eyes,
and repeats the name over and over
until it becomes a prayer. But here
the name lies empty as a hand
traced on a wall, or the scrabbled
effort of my uncle's speech as he lies
in bed, his stories a clot of gutturals
he wants us to decode, distorted
mirror he hopes will get him true.

             V.

In the poem my father never wrote,
we stand together on a long pier.
Beside us, unmoored, the sleeker ship backs free,
an embodiment of grace, into the flow.
He has shown me everything, each deck and cabin,
the ballroom with its murals and chandeliers,
the great engines that hummed to life, the huge wheel.

Off sounding—a long-held note
as it eases into the harbor, rights itself to ride
the current downstream into the Narrows
and under the flared suspension of the bridge,

24

the river swallowing its wake.
And my father leans close to tell me something,
my father leans close to me, whispering.

MY MOTHER AT THE HOUSE
OF HER FATHER'S FATHERS

Driving east from Westport in midsummer rain,
a days-long steady drizzle that dampens
her one trip back to her imagined home,
I guide our rental down unfamiliar roads
whose mirror traffic leaves her praying in back,
hands bound in her rosaries, the beads
rubbed blankly as a Croagh Patrick pilgrim's:
"Watch, Danny," and "Are you sure this is right?"
or some such warning I've heard a hundred times.
"Take it easy, Hel," my father says. Pastures
slip along the windshield's slickened lens,
my own impatience settling on me like the mists
of passing fields—cold, sodden, and resolved.

This was my idea, to arrange her return
to where she'd never been, or had been only
in the myth she made of her life, daughter
of a father she storied into legend,
the pursuing ghost of her fraught affections.
Not far from where we drive: Strokestown House
and the bronze coffin ship beside Clew Bay,
its spirit crew piloting beyond our sight
to real bodies starved to artifacts of bone.
Here is from where my mother's father hailed,
though all I remember is our ritual drives
to what seemed then a distant neighborhood,
the nursing home's halls cleansed, immaculate,
my grandfather's hand clawing mine from bed,
his deep-set eyes and stubble face, a voice
thin as memory retracing threadbare steps,
his beatings transfigured into codes of love.

Now I can almost hear his voice in the voice
of the stranger who tells us we're not far,
just back along the road there out of town

a ways beyond the Maxol, past the ruin—
Brize Castle's irreparable mound of stones—
then right up the hill of the paved *boreen.*
This was the townland of the Ruanes,
my mother's name a belling echoed back
in trespass—Helen Theresa Angelus,
resonant as the names she would compose
for girls she never had.
                              Past the proper age
for carriages, she'd wheel her sons down Third,
its bakeries, delis, dress shops—its legion
of Irish bars, blunt and ungentrified,
the bridge still unrisen above the Narrows.
She'd wheel us, too, past Visitation's walls,
where the life she didn't choose, cloistered
and virginal, murmured on without her.

Outside the car, the Mayo Plains unreel,
dubbed "To Hell or Connaught" by the defeated
banished to these stone-invested fields
among the wild, my own buried birthright
nascent in this realm through accident
of birth, historical knowledge my mother
would have little of. "That's interesting,"
she'd say, then turn back to what she knew—
a cultivated picture of her past
rehearsed in stories told on holidays,
told as lessons, truth be told, to keep us
from becoming what she could not control,
my refusal a scar among the other scars
unspoken.
                    We turn where the road emerges
past the ruin, the shrine of a holy well
at the low hill's curve, then follow the rise.
And there it is, so we believe, all gray
under the sky's mattress, gray on gray.

I pull the car over to the fuchsia hedge,
deora de, "tears of God," dripping in rain:
this house raised out of famine given flesh.
She props herself shakily against the hood
beside my father. Inside a year,
she'll be nearly dead, heart-failed, self-starved,
until she'll no longer be the woman
I'll witness withered needlessly away,
nor the over-loving mother who loved
nonetheless, but some embittered Niobe
unable to escape the gods' demands,
the razor of her last words: "I have no children"—
and see myself then as the shipwrecked son
in quest of home, taking the tests in stride,
until I descend among the shades, pour
lamb's blood on the steaming floor and find
among the lapping dead my mother there:
though it's not lamb's blood, but the womb's,
what I drank inside her body, her face
quickening beside the pool's mute image.

There's no one home. And as I walk
back to her along the gravel path,
saying this may not be the house—we saw
no name, that we'll ask further up the hill,
try another road, whatever she wants—
she waves her hand at us summarily
as though she is tossing a ball, then
lowers herself glumly into the back seat
of the still ticking car—"Forget it, let's go on."

III

BAY RIDGE

BAY RIDGE

All my dreams were of ships....

Prelude: The Narrows

"That's Dave Brown's house—do you remember?"
I feel the thin weight of my father's hand
on my arm, slow the car to Seventy-Ninth
and Shore where the two-story brick still stands,
though my father's friend is long since gone.
In his basement he kept guns, grenades,
his hat from the Spanish-American War,
the prize of a baseball signed by Babe Ruth.
All that afternoon we sat on his porch
and watched ferries churn across the harbor,
the Bridge rising slowly over the Narrows
at the round earth's imagined corners
where the Hudson opens into Gravesend.
Father, you asked if I remembered. I do.

The Avenue

French fries, burgers, baba, tabbouleh—
smells that whir through the exhaust fan of Sally's,
acrid *mélange*, the blades furred with grease,
then across the Avenue where Frances Guariglia
walks with my mother, as she does each week,
past The Hutch and Sal's Salumeria,
to Frank and Albert's Beauty Salon
while my father tends bar at The Legion:

Though if it's Sunday we're off to Mass,
the scent of danish from Lund's Bakery
tempting us as if it were the bread of life.
Even now, midway, I look back and see
the picture of a road aglow with signs—
Woods' Butcher's, Century's, Circles, Rose Glass.

A Scar

A crash that hammered through jet-black night
woke us to cries, our own, the fraught calls
of startled parents running down the hall.
Father, fumbling, flicked open the light.
So we found ourselves somehow still intact
under sheets smattered with ceiling debris
while mother hugged us tight below the rift,
soothing us, even with her whiskey breath.

Now, on holidays, when we make it home
to strained hellos, petering talk—dull ache
of what has never healed—no one
wants to set the sky crashing, or wake
those two still asleep in quicksand beds,
the plastered-over scar stark above their heads.

Broadcast

I keep tasting that clod of Brooklyn dirt
my cousin, Tony, shoved into my mouth
when I was four. I still hear his howls
as I sobbed upstairs to my parents' house,
spitting a soup black as gutter water
into the freckled basin of the sink,
then crouched under our ancient radio,
dead for decades, set on its deco table
in the hall, the polished console
like a bishop's mitre, till my mother
called from the kitchen, "It's not so bad,
why don't you sing a song?" And so I did.
And so I hear it now, low white noise
broadcast down the static of the years.

Blackout

All of us gathered on the summer-warmed roof
of Pearl Court, star-haze like milk spreading
over moldered creosote, sugar grains
of mortar—father, mother, brother, me,
grandmother dragging her regal cigarette.
We might be sailing down the Seine
in a canvas by Renoir, each of us
afloat in a floating world, its colors
garishly bright. Out over the real rail,
extinguished moons of streetlamps hover
along the Avenue dark as tar. No planes
blink flight paths overhead. Skyline's gone,
our lightship city blackened out of sight.
What if this present were the world's last night?

The Apartments

Tokeneke, Flagg Court, The Barkaloo,
The Bay Shore, The Verrazano, The View....
And out from our third floor bedroom window
you could follow the lines of rowhouse yards
to where Anastasia Court, red brick and turrets
—named after a don shot getting a haircut—
rose over the Avenue. Or maybe it was
that Russian Princess rumored still alive?

How the names call us deeper: *anastasis*,
meaning "resurrection," my own *Pearl Court*
a current running along the Narrows,
splitting off, doubling back, an undertow
riding its motions out to sea, its mark
a swirl of wind traced across the surface.

Stickball

Pock, pock.... The sound of those determined volleys
rocketing off the gray slab concrete wall
in Moon Man Park would carry half a block
to where Bobby, Tony, Bones, and I
hustled to the court we hoped we'd find,
our bats, taped broom handles, in our hands,
the pink *"Spauldeen"* squeezed and squeezed again,
as though all joy depended on the game:
to play all day and not throw out your arm;
color the box; knock one on a stinging arc
over the blown out park-house; or fasten
your fingers against the seam and let fly,
then watch the dribbling-back. A galaxy
of chalk-dust where the flung ball met its mark.

St. Anselm's

The believer does not seek to understand
that he may believe, but believes that he
may seek to understand—words of the saint
inscribed in marble above the chantry.
Counter the soritical John Shashaty
before his dismissal from seventh grade
to Sister Mary Mileetia: *Screw God.*
Stuff of legend by which we made our gods,
as though the time alone could be redeemed
by telling how we knelt at the claustral
altar, or on the Feast of St. Blaze
stretched out our necks for the murmuring priest
to bless with a cross of flaming candles
in a world composed of fire and the Word.

Long Jump Pit

Sweat pants, peach fuzz, Olympian dreams,
skin bristling in the early Autumn chill—
our gawky crew of would-be track stars
lined up at the fence-line of the schoolyard
where one by one under Coach McCartney's stare
(his steel eyes wide, peeled for "the natural")
we toed-up to the runway, launched for the pit
carved into concrete and filled with sand.

Nothing proved us but our own scarred shins,
forgotten childhood falls, the strange beating
of wings inside our guts as our arms pumped
and pumped and legs took on a life in air—
as though we were maidens chased by some swift god,
our own limbs branches crackling into bloom.

Eye-Full Tower

Where a love-dock jutted into the Narrows
I took turns with friends at a crack of light
someone scraped into the one black window
of the Eye-Full Tower, and saw through the tight
crush of men a woman dancing naked,
her sequined bridle glittering down her breasts
drenched in luminous sweat and smoke-haze.
From one she snatched a lit cigarette
and, her face blasé as a goddess's,
blew smoke-rings at the howling crowd.
I rose then to my own loneliness,
eyeing with those men what floated on a cloud:
each ring a zero dispersing in space,
the hope born of the heart's raw promise.

Barkaloo Cemetery

The way you could walk past without knowing
it was there, tucked behind its padlocked gate
at the corner of Windsor and Narrows
where the storm-fence of our school parking lot
bordered littered curbs—a forgotten shrine
to the Revolution, its brownstone graves
chipped like first teeth, the names worn clean.
And how, one night, after Mandala gave
the finger to that crowd from Owl's Head,
I hunkered down in there, asthmatic, my lungs
two fists of clenched air, where the patient dead
slept tight in their beds, and above me
blank apartment windows stared like a threat—
then a knife jutting hard against my throat.

Shore Road

The can's soft, foaming shush when you hooked
your finger inside the flip-top, music
from the school gym blaring across the road
to where we stood huddled, our jacket pockets
crammed with six-packs—*There was a lady*
we all know: Led Zeppelin and defiance.
Brothers mulling like guards outside the dance,
the girls bussed in from Fontbonne, Stella Maris....

Out through the wrought iron pickets of the park,
an unkempt thicket where no rushes grew
(only mottled diamonds, murmur of traffic
along the Belt) we'd stare out at the Narrows
between beers, boy-talk, flirting with sin.
And she's buying a stairway to heaven....

Skytop

I loved the feel of the table's green expanse,
the felt skin-tight against its level plain,
how the stark heat of the overhead lamp
beat down on your neck as you leaned
over the bunker, the cue weighed snugly
against your back hand palm, its neck sliding
down the bridge of your thumb, your squinted eye
plumbing a straight line into the pocket
having tested every angle, the rack
shattered as though at random, but governed
by precise law, your shot part choice, part fate
now measured again through the room's blue fog
that was three floors up from the humming street,
a last squeak of chalk for the moment of truth.

Brown-Eyed Girl

Where did we go days when the rain came?
To Brody's, Skinflint's, Griswold's, Tun's,
Beard's, O'Sullivan's, every bar a station
on the March of the Wooden Leg. Just back
from college, we'd plan to make our way
the thirty blocks from Three Jolly Pigeons
to the Shore, a drink in each dive. No one
ever made it, stumbling into Howe's to hear
Jack Whitman belt out his covers of Van
and The Eagles, the crowd singing along
as they did each week. And me next to you,
so richly painted, tight blue jeans, the laugh
I loved—*Do you remember when?*—like an ad
for contentment. But I was already gone.

IV

A COAT

A COAT

(for Manny Verdi)

Always it will be too big for me, this gift
    given by a friend, this old coat
        worn by his grandfather,
    threadbare, elbows torn,
the pockets two gashed lairs opening into depths.

When he jumped ship sixty years ago,
    communist, stowaway from Il Duce,
        he spoke a poor man's Genoese—
    language Dante called unsuitable
even for pigs—and settled in a sixth floor walk-up

on Hudson Street, and wore the longcoat
    he'd brought from Ciavari.
        That summer, liberated from college,
    my friend and I called ourselves
The Europa Boys, and made our scatter-shot trek

across the Old World to finish on a piazza
    overlooking the Mediterranean—
        warm bowls of coffee
    sipped alongside fishermen, my friend's people:
Uncle Nino, at seventy his arms taut as oars,

holding out one index finger to make his point,
    moustache curled under his chin
        like a Zouave; Laurencetti,
    who laughed at the names of cities: *Chicago, Sacramento,*
each a sign that flickered between a blessing and a curse.

And Paola who kept the bar beside the beach,
    who we dreamed might hold us
        to her breasts
    as if we were living *La Dolce Vita.*
And Americo, Barola, Pina, Pascolina, Un Occhio....

Names that even now my friend repeats, talismans
        of his origins that slip seamlessly
                into stories of his grandfather
        for whom the New World
was only hard labor, a place for his son to begin.

And so he went back to his hillside
        above the village, a recluse, legend has it,
                who killed his best friend
        "because it was him or me."
Here, in the myths we make of our lives,

the names lift out of their places, threads
        woven into another fabric, like the words
                that came with the others here,
        with those who left
or had to leave—*jukebox, futz, speil, poppycock, banjo.*

Giacin, grandfather of my friend, who came
        to these shores and returned
                alone, listen:
        I'm wearing America like your coat,
the body outsized and rumpled, marred by stains,

buttons loose or missing, the seams coming apart—
        a gift you'd like to give away
                but can't. And so you come
        to find it beautiful, smoothing your hand
along its length, the frayed stitches, the pattern of small bones.

A LIFE NOT LIVED

(Summer 1980—for Michael Hardiman)

Remember those all night *seisuns*, hiking
the six miles back from Dun Laoghaire
after the bus lines shut down, having gotten,
as we quipped, "Dun Laoghaireous,"
on rounds of Paddy's and Guinnesses?
We'd lace our thick Brooklyn tongues
with Barry Fitzgerald brogues,
roaring through Booterstown, Black Rock
till we reached our digs behind gates
of the Christian Brother's Provincialite,
ducking the shuffle for sunrise Mass.
Grown up on Tet and the Ugly American,
we'd have purged ourselves like dockside *boke*.

What we wanted was a life not lived,
emigré bloodlines flooding back to origins—
two green *culchees* mad for the city,
its pubs, bed-sits, black pools of history,
Dublin decked out in raw loveliness
like that Northside tinker *aisling*
who lifted her skirt for our benefit.
Cut off, we'd have longed for the good life,
those seaside estates and guzzling Caddies,
skyscrapers, Stetsons, gruff private eyes
flashed nightly on satellite RTE
from the promised land of opportunity
that's glossy and golden and inadequate.

PALLBEARERS AT EMILY DICKINSON'S FUNERAL

Death but the Drift of Eastern Gray
Dissolving into Dawn away,
Before the West Begin—

She died at sunset facing west,
her own society
this room—her soul—its offing
a vastness like the sea

these six endured on coffin ships,
her bark their burden now,
in her hands two heliotropes
whose mind was measured noon.

Each Consciousness must Emigrate.
Her passage stayed at home,
while these stalwarts made literal
the crux of their *immram*

through swells of gray immensity,
their terms in remnant holds,
and wakes distilled their ecstasies
until they fathomed here.

Now horizon is this transit
admitted by the train
that passes through her rose estates
into unstopped expanse.

They bear her single privacy
surpassed, as coal to pearl—
the center and circumference
cracked open like a seal.

The meadow opens through the gate,
a Paradise of Now,

where cricket consorts play the bones
above the undertow.

Incense of apple blossom drifts
with bell notes in the trees—
and resurrection's skiffs embark
at dew's velocity.

AT THE LOWER EAST SIDE TENEMENT MUSEUM

As emigration from east to west followed the latitude,
so does the foreign influx in New York distribute itself
along certain well-defined lines.... A map of the city colored
to designate nationalities, would show more stripes than the skin
on a zebra, and more colors than a rainbow...

Crowded as we are we might be trooping down a passage
to the dead center of Cheops, not this hallway, cave-lit,
haunted by pastoral oils painted in circles on the wall.

Peel back the wallpaper, the plaster covered in burlap,
and the tenement becomes a palimpsest of lives,
the mind a flicker-box of moving pictures, like thumbed

stills the walls animate: a panorama of fire-escapes,
handshakeshafts where light filters down, a minor grace,
to lie like fine dust on faces bored and anonymous, bored

and frightened, or trying to shine with muted hope
behind the filmy panoply of windows. Dickens saw them,
coarse and bloated looks with counterparts the world over,

patched windows scowling dimly, these narrow ways reeking
everywhere with dirt and filth, his genius visiting on each
only the masks of the time; though in these cluttered mazes,

alleys heaped with ash-cans, rags, bannered by flapping
laundry, the air imbued with the stoops' cacophonies,
Whitman discerned "the native grand opera of America."

Clatter of wheelhub. Hawkers' calls. The blunt tap
of a shoemaker's hammer. An organgrinder's Turkish March.
Ram's horn. Zither. The sweatshop's low, unmodulated hum.

And now from one blighted court—Gotham, or Bandit's Roost—
a crowd of toughs stares back, growlers in high-button coats
and bowler hats, emerged from their garrets: "Swamp Angels,"

"Pug-Uglies," crossmen and crackmen of "the Bloody Old Sixth"
flash-talking in a fade-out of sunlight off the roofs,
heading for a bender in Cats Hollow or Paradise Square,

hot for the hot corn girls on Little Water, Squeeze Gut Alley.
A blind man sells pencils outside Broome Street Looking Glass.
Newsboys shoot craps behind the Children's Aid Lodging House.

Kneeling beside her wicker basket, perched against an iron rail,
the stale bread vendor holds a sabbath loaf shaped like a wreath.
Shoeless boys huddle on a sidewalk grate. There are pigs' feet

cooking in the *crubeen* for the rag-picker, for the coal-heaver,
stains indelible on the cigarmaker's fingers,
a jigsaw of horse-carts, coal-carts, rag-carts, and fruit-carts.

There are runners hustling hoards from the slips and wharves
to the five-cent spots on Bayard, the seven-cent cots on Pell.
There is whipworm, T.B., cholera ("the scourge of God"),

the outhouse, the House of Industry, and the House of Blazes.
There is Jewtown, Chinatown, Little Dublin, and Little Africa,
the brick-in-your-eye ignorance of Draft Riot and Know-Nothing.

But down in the dance halls and black-and-tan dives of The Bend,
in Peter Williams' and The Diving Bell, the throngs gather
for the red-faced trumpeter who looks like he's blowing glass,

an invisible wall of sound bubbling out into the street;
and the man whose feet move quickly as fingers on a tambourine—
single-shuffle, double-shuffle, cut and cross-cut, the steps

a ripple of waves that fold into each other in low-ceilinged smoke:
a joining of jig and juba. Or like those lovers in the corner,
their skins blending in the half-light of the world to come.

THE OTHER HALF

(Jacob Riis, 1849-1914)

When the well-to-do were sleeping
in their uptown beds, I prowled
the roosts and hovels of the poor
hauling my cyclops camera
into every flyblown tenement
from Five Points to Chatham Street
to cut my newsman's teeth on portraits
of the other half crowded in bunks,
or huddled alone in tramp's nests,
wretched as the rags hawked from carts.

Dirt and desolation. Darkened wells
where the rent collector's knocks
stammer from cellar to attic room.
Through these firetraps I made
my own midnight rounds, hungry
to shock the privileged from their dream
of gardens and lace, the slumlord
from his pious indignation,
to light the lives of the common horde,
and rested my case with the governor.

I had been there myself, blank face
in a station house hall, staring
from a line-up of vagrants and thugs.
No work for the immigrant, white
as I was, from Copenhagen,
thrown in with the like of Joss and Jew,
Negro, Italian, Teuton, and Paddy.
Three years I traffic'd with boot-blacks,
coal-heavers, my clothes silvered
with the spindrift of ash-bins.

I rose from all that, like a man self-saved,
and made my own indignant descent
to bear witness to the waste,
the upas tree of capital and greed.
These pictures—Street Arabs asleep,
Swamp Angels in their lair, those boys
fetching growlers of beer—bring back
a history, foretell what never ends:
the light ignited at my pistol's crack,
some child's eyes blinding in the flash.

THE COUNTRY

(In memory of Robert Kirkpatrick, killed 2/26/93)

We called it "The Country" and it was.
Those summer Fridays after work
my favorite uncle, Bob, would drive
from Brooklyn to his five room bungalow
on a postage stamp of ground by Crandon Lake.
He loved that house, fixed it board by board,
sawed and leveled, joined, planed, and painted
until what he'd made had matched his wish.
And we loved driving there with him,
my brother and I, piling into the Bug,
then riding out over the Narrows, over
the gleaming bridge built in our lifetime,
that nameless mansion on Todt Hill
our midway marker to the Turnpike,
its stench of chemical and slaughterhouse,
its refinery stacks like votive candles.
Whippany, Hope, Netcong, Sparta, Swartzwood—
the names fled past on the new interstate
into signs on roads of diminished light.
At the last mile, winging down the long hill
overlooking the lake, he'd shut the engine,
the headlights, open all the windows.
We'd glide to the driveway by the moon alone.

      ℘

Here, too, even before we came, the lots
had been divided, the cut-out homes
propped on hillsides, scaled into squares.
And still, fleeing city neighborhoods
like the other weekend pioneers,
I could almost imagine virgin woods
as I explored swamps, thickets, discovered

56

deer bones in the backyard, or coming back
from play saw my uncle and aunt, framed
by light of the kitchen window, the house
hovered over by darkening birches.

℘

For years, at Christmas in my parents' house,
he'd oblige the crowd of family
by crooning his version of Moon River
into his scotch and soda, my aunts, my mother,
laughing as their husbands drowned each other
in background vocals tuneless as radios
scrambling through stations. I remember
nightlong, my uncle cracked walnuts,
squeezing each shell between his thumb
and finger till the tough pith snapped,
its trove falling into his palm. "You try,"
he'd say, and laugh as I pressed hard,
my face flushing, the nut unbreakable
as a diamond, until his hand cupped mine,
clamped down vise-tight,
and I'd feel the stone pop.
Those times I might have been his son
when he'd show me how to throw the curve,
his strikeout pitch in the minors,
or when he'd tell us how he fought in Korea,
squinting his eyes to make us laugh,
a sit-com schtick that went no further
—"I'm the original Archie Bunker"—
as he smiled and turned away. In years since,
I could still see his ruddy face aglow
under citronella torches on his patio
long after he sold the house, moved upstate
from the neighborhood, my memory of him

fading to a white shine, like that picture
I took of him as he took mine, everything
above the neck cancelled in the flash.

             ℘

On the morning of the explosion, my aunt
waving from the screen door, TV voices
from inside flung against February air,
my uncle backs his pick-up from the driveway,
flicks on the country station, rides out
his winding side street to the Thruway,
then along the Hudson and the Palisades:
Pearl River, Tappan, Tenafly, Fort Lee.
The silver plank of the bridge juts
fantastically from cliffs, the cross-hatched
girders of its towers rising over the site
of the defunct amusement park, its slogan,
Come on Over, a huckster's parody
of words carved in stone above the harbor.
As traffic slows crossing the bridge,
maybe he muses looking out at the river,
admiring its slow expansion against stone,
the cruise ships lulling at midtown docks,
the vaulting skyscraper where he works.
He wouldn't linger over the island in mist
where my great aunt was turned back
seventy years before, where his own people
came, mingling streams of German, Scots—
You should love this country or leave it.
Lunchtime underground: the garage
suspended like a womb in bedrock,
the world above a gleaming crystal
of glass and steel. I see him
in mid-joke—the one about the parrot

58

and the black man—his eyes squinting slyly
anticipating the punch line, when it hits.

℘

Now, he's a public image, adrift in space,
a sensational headline, SIX KILLED
BY TERROR BOMB, his face shocked white
at the bottom of a crater the talk show host
begged my aunt to witness on camera,
for the ratings wars. He's the wedding photo
flashed on the news, the presidential letter
on the family shrine, not the man who held
my brother and me in laughing headlocks
that blinding day at the country fair,
all strong-armed play and bruising innocence,
but a carved name on a monument, an American.

THE ISLAND

A generous race, and strong to dare
With hearts as true as purest gold
With hands to soothe as well as strike...

What I remember most are the surgical scars
on the man's neck, whiter than the rest of him,
like touch-up paint, or the faintest slashes
of bark on a healed-up tree. From them
the rest of the scene takes shape—
how he sat neighborly in my cousin's backyard,
his Caribbean-blue shirt splashed with palms
spreading over his gut as he chain-smoked,
each cigarette dispersing among us
as we gathered around the picnic table, a clique
of men and boys left to themselves while the women
attended a daughter's bridal shower.

We had driven, my mother, father, and I,
by a usual route, avoiding the streets
of certain neighborhoods, brick slabs of projects,
tenements, battered brownstones, the dark faces
we'd been brought up to fear: men gathered on stoops
or—so we might have imagined—milling around corners,
a heavy bass beat spilling out of car windows,
storefronts, across the fractured tundra of vacant lots.
And since we'd never been to that house before,
we were warned, off the parkway, to keep
to the avenue, to follow the lights past Junction
where the streets changed to become safe and familiar.
"This is an island," another neighbor remarked,
"the blacks are all around us." And in no time
the whole company gave their version of the state
of things, how they were the last hold-outs
of a better time as my father and I listened quietly,
for by then I had learned when not to speak—

60

though I had seen him look his own neighbor
in the eye when my brother brought his friend,
Michael, home from college: "No one tells me
who to have in my house." And I'd witnessed
my mother's nervous kindness as she lifted
my finger from a delivery man's hand. But by then
my cousin's scarred friend had chimed in: "Down South
they knew what to do with their niggers." And soon
it was the same brutal story in earnest—a man dragged
pleading at night from his home, the rest of the town
sleeping, the man beaten and hung from a tree.

To picture those men now is to see a negative,
white faces charred to the image they hate,
until the past cuts like my father's words
that evening driving home, "A good bunch of guys,"
or the laughter that swallowed us all after the women
came back, and the bride-to-be showed off her gifts,
and my cousin and the scarred man fired up the grill.

LOST GARDEN ELEGIES

Shuttles in the rocking loom of history....

I.

My alley wasn't Paradise but Pearl,
its courtyard a concrete square
where wrought iron fire-escapes
connected earth to sky. The time
I brought my friend from school,
bussed in from another neighborhood,
we felt the building's walls of eyes
shadow above us like hungry birds.

II.

The chocolate man wheeling meat
   into Woods' Butchers
laughs when I touch his skin
   to see if he's real.

Echoing off the spotless white counter:
   my mother's stuttered laughter
as she takes my hand away, the silence
   of the owners with their knives....

III.

Who is that boy about my age
saluting his father in the box

62

marines lift from the open hearse
on our big black-and-white TV?
Why does my mother cry and cry
in the haze of our apartment rooms?
Why does my father look so glum?
And why am I bored, bored all day?

What did the radio just say
as Mother packs me off to school?
Another dead. A brother dead.
Here is the man in the candy store,
his hand shaking my change to me.
Here is the nun with a TV set
for the lesson on living history.
To the Asian dead we'll add this name.

And where am I when James Earl Ray
captures the third inside his scope?
What do the neighborhood men say
in barber shop, in corner bar?
"They finally got the bastard—good."
And here is my father, threading hooks
to hang new drapes in the living room
ring after ring, links in the chain.

IV.

Eenee meenee minee mo.
Catch a nigger by the toe.
If he hollers let him go.
Eenee meenee minee mo.

And if he's mine
  you bring him back.
And if he's yours
  I'll fetch the rack.
And if he's mean
  we'll kill the buck.

"Wasn't it a tiger?"

And if he screams
  they'll be too late
to heal the wounds
  of Runagate—
No "Fly Away Home"
  or Jesus rest.

"Daddy where's the tiger?"

Eenee meenee minee mo.
You will reap what you will sow.
One is coal, the other snow.
Look, the tiger's caught the toe.

V.

In our kitchen's cigarette fog,
among the clatches of uncles and aunts
who crowded our apartment each Christmas,
I never saw her face or heard her name.
Only once, by casual reference,
did my father mention her, wistfully:
in the back of the church at his wedding,

64

cast off by the family, the wild sister
whom he hadn't seen in thirty years.
Over time stories surfaced like debris—
her getting "knocked up," selling her child;
and, worst, running away with her black lover.
Throwback to a time of jig and juba,
to black-and-tan dives—"White Negroes,"
"Smoked Irish".... My lost cousins
pass by me darkly on these streets,
our pasts sprayed in dazzling colors
on a tenement wall, whitewashed and hushed.

VI.

José, Randy, Shawn—
three boys living an American Dresden:
burnt-out skulls of buildings,
drug-dealers and their dogs,
the nuns in dish-towel habits
serving the "poorest of the poor,"
that broken glass mosaic of a park....

Silent José beside the chain-link fence,
in his baggy pants, still the fastest
kid in camp; Randy with his mother,
needle tracks along her arms, a riot
of anger in his eyes; Shawn, his wit quick
as his bat ("Your mother has more chins
than the Chinese phone directory"),
teasing me from my awkwardness
that first working summer in college—
days I'd drive from my walled island

to this otherworld, becoming less other
until, one night, my car broken down,
the projects hovered above me,
and someone shouted *Hey white boy*
from a passing van, and I waited,
counting each minute for the tow.
No taxi would take me
from that desolate corner until, unbidden,
a stranger stood beside me, hailed
a speeding cab and told the driver,
"You take this young man home."

VII.

Mark, the *X*'s on our uniforms
(insignia for a patron saint)
symbolized more to you than me.

I could trace the cipher of my name
to horse thieves back in County Cork,
so one loquacious uncle quipped.

Such family trees were lost to you
whose name was latinized in chains—
Radix, "root," whom you had to become.

In circles we'd pace around the track
to goad ourselves, as if hurdling were
the outward trial of our fraught homes.

Our practices—taut ballet stretches,
grueling sets—fashioned us gazelles
for the pistol's crack at weekend meets

where I crouched at the relay's mark,
while you cleared the line of barriers
toward me before you shouted *Go!*

And I broke free of my own blocks
as if the world depended on it.
Not great, not bad, those answering flights....

AFTERMATH

(9/11/01)

It will not be
how the saint imagined,

the soul distilling
into what comes after

the way a woman
wades into ocean

that laps her skin
at body temperature

so she feels herself
the waves' completion,

a fluency
of wine in water,

her body all flow
as she slides under

then out of herself
like a silk nightgown

though you wish it so,
though you wish it so.

Instead, these ashes
through the flood-lit night,

through the silent heaven,
rising, rising....

A MOSQUE IN BROOKLYN

There is no prayer that can abolish history,
though in this basement mosque the muezzin's history

gathers in his throat like a tenor's aria
and he calls to God to put an end to history.

From my courtyard room I hear his song ascending,
the divine name whirling its rebuke to history—

Allah, Allah—above the crowded rowhouse roofs.
Their rusted antennas, stalled arrows of history,

would transmit a daily riot of talk and news,
the world boxed inside a glowing square of history.

I've seen them on the street, the faithful in their robes
walking along store-fronts, a different history

clothing them, like me, in our separate skins,
though here we are at the scope-end of history:

Goodness is timeless, the great English poet wrote,
and not just for himself—the crime is history.

But as if to prove the old Sufi fable true
these prayers are lifted on the thermals of history,

and sound strangely like that congregation of birds;
no, the remnant who survived a blighted history,

having stayed their quest into the final valley
where a Great Tree rose, its branches thick as history.

And there they lost themselves, flourishing into the One
without division, without names, without history.

V

AT THE TREE OF MANY,
ONE

AT THE TREE OF MANY, ONE

I.

Behind our house in Grossi's single field,
  the sun slides below cedars,
    sky tilted to dusk.
    All day I've played
    in junkyard, shale-pit,
  darted through woods with a plastic rifle,
  till now, waist-deep in blowing grass,
I stop shock-still at the sound of my name.
At this moment you might have fled us,
    called back from our games
    at the snub-end of summer,
or driven like a catkin through the quickening air.

II.

    Who called me back
    was not my mother,
    who lay in her bed
in the hospital overlooking the Narrows.
Where she heard the doctor's words,
"She came too soon, we couldn't save her...."
Outside her window: bridge-lights
    suspended in fog,
a string of pearls her nurse said.
So years later my mother confessed to me,
her voice thin as thread through a needle's eye.

III.

Colleen Regina. Kathleen Ann.
Names bestowed on wished-for lives....
  Those late nights in our kitchen,
  my father asleep, my brother gone
    from that house's angers,
    I listened as she nursed
    another drink to stories
of dolls and shopping, braided hair,
    a daughter close as a sister—
    the ideal world she created
  in a haze of regrets, how always
  a mother loses her sons.
In those hours you became a thought
  almost palpable, a hint of smoke
    drifted from her cigarette,
or a soul's spark poised for release.

IV.

Once, an ancient hymn recounts, a child
  travels from his father's house
    to rescue a single pearl
  guarded by a serpent in the sea.
Putting off his robe of glory, the boy
    descends into Egypt,
  and as happens in such stories,
  forgets the purpose of his quest,
 seduced by customs of an alien land—
though like clockwork comes the awakening:
the pearl saved, his inheritance restored.

But why does the child leave at all?
　　And what's the worth of a pearl
　for a house so surfeited with wealth?
So we renounce the myth, turn from it
　　the way tourists turn
　from beggars; say meaning moves
　from life to life without a trace,
so when we come to the end it is this truth
　　we see: the serpent
　coiled around a black hole.
And you who never left, who have no need
　of stories, what knowledge
　　can you give us who pause
　　on the journey outward
only to feel inside the drag of created things?

V.

In the beginning: an atom of time,
　atom of space, flung gasses,
　　I see you, sister,
　　lured back in return—
　fetus, fish, single-cell, nil.
There, in those final waters,
　　you are again
what we can no longer be:
　　uncreated, an absence
from which even God's hand emerges.

VI.

The Time Capsule
   on our bookshelf
   took up two shelves.
Each night I'd pick a year
to pour over pictures
of a century's events.
   This was history,
quickened by a whiff of mildew:
   Kitty Hawk rising
over Carolina dunes, depression
breadlines, trenches at Verdun,
   an era's assorted portraits;
   on the couch our father
watching television, who survived
   Guam, Leyte Gulf, the pier
   explosion at Luchenbach
where he woke with his friend lying
   dead on top of him
   the year before I was born,
   the dock's air
   thick with voices of the dead
summoning their one prayer of reversal,
   the way the Narrows' surf
   seethes in its breakers:
what if, what if, what if, what if....
   What pursues me? Everything
      you've missed.

VII.

That I am, that I am—there's no sorrow
  greater, the contemplative said,
than to feel this "naked spark of being":
  and so he leaves his name
to our unknowing. Yet this self-taste,
  how vividly it stung the poet
  until he saw in everything—
windhover, ploughman, poplar, wreck—
  the charge of mastering grandeur.
  Height and length and breadth,
  all that gives shape to this earth,
  must be put behind a cloud, must be
  forgotten, with every creature,
  for you will not be perfect in love
  until this too is destroyed.
  To what purpose then do we long
  to preserve the illusion,
this real earth, we who are not like you,
  who would make our lives
  leaves pressed deeply into a book
that cures and keeps and heals our memory?

VIII.

Sister, those stone walls, overrun by ferns,
that divided each field, come back to me.
And the Narrows, its freighters sounding
  through thickest fog. This world
calls like a neighbor through the dusk.
Again the wind steps over your soul.

VI

PEARL COURT

PEARL COURT

To inhabit onerically the house we were born in
means more than to inhabit it in memories; it means
living in the house that is gone, the way we used
to dream in it...

I. The House

Here, where the paved ridge declines
into the bay, I keep coming back
to this building, its blunt facade
of storied brick, latticed fire-escapes,
a monument to function—mortar box
some dull architect raised above farms
dwindling like crossroads or whistle-stops,
the city's raw flow sprawling eastward

to the Island, block on block of apartments,
row houses crowded to pristine lawns
along the shore—though I loved
the wrought iron doors outside the foyer,
between each grille a painted-over flower,
on every pane of glass a scratched-in name
or emblem embossed in magic marker
to preserve a life from the recordless.

Carved plaster. Affectations of marble.
The long hallway devoid of furniture
where I'd hurl my *"Spauldeen"* at plaster,
hearing its report echo up the floors.
I'd watch for Mr. Johnson, the landlord,
on patrol in his great brown coat,
who changed his name from the Greek.
Now, stiff as washed-up actors at a call,

the others come, passing from the numbered

honeycomb of their rooms: Astrid
and Gunnar, crew-cut jutting off his head,
his hands a prizefighter's. His wife, her breath
redolent with drink, would slip me quarters
on the stairs. Frances and Tony lived
above the alley, their door always ajar.
Tuscanies of sauce drifted into the hall

with smoke from Tony's panatellas.
Each week they'd play Po-Ke-No, Frances
calling the cards, her rough contralto
throaty as Bacall's. And "Skinny Jeannie,"
who would hunt the avenue for bargains.
She'd coif her hair to a stiffened hive, brag
of her virginity. Madeleine lived upstairs,
a French page-boy and porcelain face.

She looked a nun and talked of nothing
but finding a husband. Old Mr. Walsh
who limped since the War. The man
called "The Farmer" who stalked the yard
with his owlish stare. Bobby Carney
who came back from Vietnam, Mother said,
"a little off." Crazy Kathryn who sang
show tunes in the hall. My own family

pent in our four rooms. I can see us all
climbing the last flight to the roof
the night the city turned blank as a screen.
In that blackness, the stars visible
above our cramped antennas, everyone
went quiet. We listened to ships sounding
on the Narrows like voices through a wall—
the muffled promise of lives beyond our own.

II. My Grandmother's Apartment

A slow air's modulated hush
gathers to jig and reel—
John Gibbons' pressed accordion
propped on his wooden leg,
his face puffed fat as a peony
above his buttoned mustard collar
and green serge coat,
his eyes flagrantly bright.
Whenever he'd arrive
I'd follow him from the foyer,
rapt with his hampered walk,
then sit at his feet staring
at the false limb in disbelief
while the rest of the family
kept time around the table,
their feet tapping out rhythms
on scuffed linoleum.
Clachan music. Riffs of her past
my mother's mother carried over
from the lost hearth. Each day,
home after school, I'd make
my visitation, sit with her
in the darkened kitchen
as her fingers clicked
through her rosary, her lips
tremulous with prayer.
Then, awash in the ritual,
I'd fetch us crullers
from Sally's Luncheonette
as she put on the kettle.
On her bedroom dresser she kept
a ceramic bust of Christ
with his right hand pointing

to the crown of his sacred heart
and its ring of flames, a secret
compartment in back that held
holy water and chrism,
her plain wooden crucifix
with its soldered Jesus,
she'd say, for when He takes me.
Now I come back to this house,
with nostalgia for tea and sweets
shared in dimly-lit rooms,
for a promise of life eternal
sculpted in tacky shrines,
to praise one-legged men
with squeeze boxes
that open and close like fans,
or like a blacksmith's bellows
to raise from the emptiness song.

III. Hope Chest

Hard to believe we could neglect it so,
year after year the sleek wood blistering
where we'd arranged the potted plants to drink
their ration of water and fitful light.
Hard to believe, though we had done the damage,
the pasts that we would keep alive in there—
old infants' clothes, old cards, old albums stacked
like ziggurats, neat rows of plastic bags
that spill a flood of photographs
at the least mishandling. I see those faces
jumbled across my childhood floor and find
among them younger versions of myself,
propped with my brother at a blanket's edge,
or at the mirror pretending to shave.
In others, I'm in my black prom tux,
cock of the walk, my arm around my girl;
or standing at the brink of Millbrook Glen,
wild-haired, drowned in my self-regard.
What did my father feel the night he wrote
this one love letter my mother kept
after the war? And what did she feel
unfolding the crisp leaf that nearly crumbles now?
Yellowed shots of a place called Shepherd's Farm,
an album that plays its sentimental march,
could be emblems of a time preserved,
though everything we know insists such tropes
don't fit, refuse the claims of changelessness.
And so those two posed together close,
twenty years younger than I am now,
appear to me a puzzle to compare
with the parents I loved and tried to know,
who lived their lives together mostly sad.
Like churned-up clay my mother's wedding dress

floats with the wreckage of this cedar box,
the gown itself a shifting confluence,
its veil ephemeral as the scent it brings
of mothballs and old wood, or some deeper past
that drifts away from me and out of sight.
I bury my face in its swell, and draw breath.

IV. Inheritors

I meet them in the hall that as a child
I claimed my own, or on landing or on stair,
where we nod hello then go our separate ways;
I to my aging parents' rooms, and them
outside to greet their own family and friends
and walk along the avenue, and browse
the changed shops—Tarantella or Autumn Leaf—
that have come to name their familiar world.

My mother's mother lived in A-4, her door
open every evening after work,
the bottle open, too, on the table
for anyone who wanted to come in.
Who followed her the summer that she died
to make her three cramped rooms their own,
or those spinster cousins who lived upstairs?
Someone else's mother, someone else's son.

When I come back these few days every year
from the other life I've made, my parents
seem a remnant of some diminished tribe,
and give their best *It's good to have you home*,
though mostly everyone they knew is gone.
The numbers mark new faces at each door
while four blocks down the Narrows shambles on.
One time it seemed that I was always here.

V. Bridge View

The grandeur of the tower was nothing at first
but our surmise at what it would become,
gleaned from rumors; though before long
we watched the stanchions' gradual ascent
above Shore Road's distant stand of trees
where Third narrowed to its vanishing point.

Nothing at first, and then, from the corner,
one day we saw the legs barely risen,
two sheer columns of iron and steel:
the tensile thighs of a man being built
foot by lifted foot from the bottom up,
girder and crossbeam, rivet and plate.

For two years he grew, his height accruing
like a child's stature notched on a wall,
while up from the Narrows the body took form
from foot to hips and vaulted crotch. But where
was the rest of him, broad torso and head?
It was we who gave that image to the air,

gave it likewise to its twin across the strait
before they strung the cables, hung the roadway
amazingly into place, so that, that first time,
we drove through a space left by torn-down homes
up the approach, the Island spread before us,
the river below, and climbed into the sky.

VI. Back Window

Down in the courtyard the Super's daughter works
her spade into ground packed tightly as cement.
Black clumps spill heavily where she leans over
like some stooped peasant of the Borinage
Van Gogh might have charcoaled into form,
though her designer jeans are pure Bay Ridge,

pure everywhere, since we've become each other,
or everyone's become us: those golden arches
I saw in Freiberg once, their plastic *M*
wrought amidst medieval stone on the *platz*;
that Kenyan chief on TV surfing the Net,
tribal robes lit by his PC's claustral glow;

or the smile of a geisha flashing her Visa—
We're everywhere you want to be. And yet,
below, this woman breaks earth as though
she tilled the land her parents left in Greece,
or some grubbed plot out of my own past,
those potato diggers in Mayo and Cork

prying blackened tubers from the ground
before the rush of their American wakes.
For as long as I can recall, every fall
it's the same. The family cuts their *drills*,
and every spring new shoots line the lot
under the drawn-down blinds of this house.

VII. Prospect

I climb the last flight to the roof and lean on the sill.
Even now this could be a separate world, smell of tar
rising in heat waves off the building's gray expanse,
the paper tacky under foot, a few listing antennas
ranged along the masonry's edge, arrows stilled in space,
their rusted poles bleeding into brick, the clipped wires
splayed like the feelers of some insect long extinct.
I used to come up here to sit and think, to read,

or look down the street to Anastasia Court, wrought iron
and turrets, as though it were the battlements
of the don they named it for; then up the avenue
to where the city rose in steel beyond the parkway,
and rises still on its raft of glass embrasures
between two rivers whose tides mark their own time
along the rotting timbers of abandoned piers
that jut like Roman oars into the water.

Heaving past Sandy Point and Gravesend into the Narrows
they come, led by tugs under the gray bow of the bridge,
tanker, liner, cargo boat and barge; then heave out again
past the grain bins of Red Hook, the slopes of Owl's Head.
Goodbye Bedloe's Island, Castle Garden that dangled
like a pocketwatch from Manhattan, its land absorbed
with the hordes who crowded here; goodbye Lightship,
the bridge tower rising where the clipper veered

from shore; veered, and became the floating palace
my grandmother boarded at Cobh, latecomer
to this "New Island" where all was flowing,
and flows on—images flashed in celluloid.
Now, out across the Narrows, a brown haze is floating
over Snug Harbor, Arthur Kill, the Kill Van Kull,

90

a spume from the refineries in Linden, Elizabeth,
the clouds dissipating west over Fords and Edison.

Here, a mite scurries on mortar grainy as salt,
joins the swarm that whirls in its orderly chaos
along the sill, a choreography of wants,
then disappears into brick. Neighborhood
or townland, where we are holds us in its prospect
until what was vision becomes what we've seen,
our flimsy antennas quicken underground, signals
coming through, voices within voices resonant in glass.

VII

THINKING OF
MEADE MOUNTAIN

THINKING OF MEADE MOUNTAIN

(for Kevin Tobin)

Kevin, last night looking out my window
at this inland sea we oddly call a lake,
the moon pouring down white light like snow
that rippled across its pliant surface,
I found myself miles from the crippled prose
of student papers—sentences like tracks
left in a wilderness of intentions—
spooled back by the tide to the ride we took

years ago along the Hudson, the used
Volkswagen you bought from our uncle
taking the serpentine turns of the Saw Mill
up river to the heart of the Catskills,
the roadway flowing under a rust-hole
in the floor. There, too, though we didn't speak
of it, a lost past pooled in exit signs—
Mohegan, Mohonk, Chappaqua, Napanoch,

the neat subdivisions glimpsed through a haze
of trees standing on once-sacred ground.
Back then, I had already stumbled on
my own *Narrow Road to the Deep North*
spurred by my adolescent faith in you,
Basho's journey an endless going forth
I'd stuffed into my pack "to light my days"
as we drove that morning to Dharmadhatu,

its shrine raised at the foot of Meade Mountain.
No moon-faced Buddhas smiled from the walls
of that monastery's enlightened halls
the way they did Saturdays in Chinatown
when we walked with our parents along streets
crowded with trinket shops where common talk
filled the air like exotic smells, two boys
dazzled in a film without sub-titles.

I was dazzled still when you led me inside,
shoes off, listening to the otherworldly hum
of monks chanting under an ether dome
of incense and prayer-wheels, mandalas hung
on whitewashed walls, a gallery of gods
and demons, and the zigzag labyrinth
of some elaborate cosmic game board
where the self moves through realms of desire

until, at the center, no movement, no self.
Nights in my room I'd listen to crickets
clamorous in field grass, each clipped song
a pure longing, the length of my legs
stiff from sitting in the buzzing half-light
hour after hour, my thoughts thick as locusts
swarming around the rhythm of my breath—
though I would be the prince Siddhartha,

his body straight and supple as a lotus,
his mind still as the space inside a vase.
Pent in my husk, I didn't last three days.
But that one afternoon, bored as I was,
I wandered outside beyond the grounds
to find myself unlatching the gate
to the dirt road that led up Meade Mountain.
And there I was, as though I'd struck out alone

along a trail we'd cut through Stillwater Woods
where we clambered together over rock walls,
on the lookout for snakes, and whacked to chaff
each overhang and bush, each subtle growth.
Coming back each day we'd follow the path
to the swamp pool where you spotted that skull
we prized for years on our bedroom shelf—
some lost dog, though we imagined it a wolf;

and imagined ourselves explorers
drawn as by divine call to the unknown:
that shed we found in the middle of nowhere,
in its dank hole a nest of robin's eggs.
Part way up the mountain I thought of that place
while I rested on cinderblocks of a house
wholly gone, its foundation upholstered
with tufts of moss, each crevice a lair.

And thought, too, of the novice Milarepa
ordered by his teacher to build a tower
only to tear it down a hundred times,
a hundred times to build it up again
until, his great will broken, he saw
as through the master's eyes who he was,
or as though the eye alone could see itself,
and sat among the rubble, and laughed:

An image so unlike the suffering Christ
I peered at through the dust-blown window
of that chapel I came to up the road,
ramshackle, its weathered shingles cracked,
breeding white cocoons of gypsy moths.
As forlorn as he looked he brought me back
to St. Anselm's, some nun's bruising fists,
Jesus gazing down, suspended from his cross

above the blackboard, his pallid flesh torn
as in our Easter songs—*O bleeding head*
so wounded with crown of piercing thorns.
It's a wonder our parents wondered why
you left the faith, finding that prince who cut
his throat to save a starving tiger's life
more your vision of how things ought to be—
no fuss, no groans—the pure equanimity

of Yeats's stone-eyed climbers in the face
of all that dread, no anguished Christ
in the olive-rich groves of Gethsemane,
nor an over-ripe existentialist like me
who brooded alone and read too much Camus.
It's the look I see still when I see you
coming back to us from your shrine room
where I imagine a million *yugas* spread

before your eyes, the years a hall of mirrors
crystalline, perfected in your perfect sight.
It's not what I saw when I reached the peak
of Meade Mountain, just meadow and forest
of this world spreading out before me—
which is what I see now when I try to read
beyond this fog to the lake's horizon
and that sailboat fading steadily from shore,

its mast like the Japanese sign for life.
Here, casinos of the Potowatomi
blink in neon along the interstate.
Gunshots rack the streets at night. We long,
you and I, for another world among
the many, one composed of light,
this universe a droplet in the sea
whose waves ride waves into transparency.

VIII

HOME IN TRANSIT

ACCORDING TO LEGEND

(Dublin, Ireland 1988)

If you wish on the outstretched hand
of the mummified crusader
buried under St. Michan's Church
your dream, as in tall tales, will come true.

I crowded down that basement years ago
with the curious, the dragged-along,
in my knapsack the notebook packed with lines,
grasped a finger, rehearsed the signs.

There's no end to this looking back, wishing for.
Faithful hand, tanned to a saint's hide,
can you feel the grip of words
fastened on you still?

A CHALK PRIMAVERA ON EDEN QUAY

(Dublin, Ireland)

Amazing it's been cribbed to the least detail,
    as though the pavement's sullen *tabula*
      woke to the dream of its own Uffizi

this busker Botticelli—his velvet hat
    propped for contributions—has brought to life
      in a rainbow tour de force of softest stone.

Here, too, crowds of nymphs and tritons announce
    the arrival of the goddess on her shell
      demure as ever, a swirl of golden hair

Cascading where waves, fluid promenade,
    deliver her as from some forties flick
      into the splendor of a fantasy.

A million ghosts step over her like air
    who lined this river once, and did for years,
      and who long gone are buried elsewhere now.

Though beauty is also an emigré,
    a face floating dumbfounded from the source,
      until the downpour descends like a hand

that wipes the palette clean—a sand painting
    some visionary washes from his sight,
      or the earth erased in a bloom of light.

BALLSBRIDGE, DARK NIGHT

I.

A woodpecker's machine gun beak
ratatats me from sleep, driving on
at its obsessive labors like
my worst self going at the Tree
of Life, desperate augers
boring for the core. Last night

I felt the old wound surge,
a thrumming at first as I sat alone,
knowing no one here, the big emptiness
nothing fills soon laying siege
until it was at my throat—
the world-keen, fierce, abject, wordless

that, expressed, devolves into cliché
or wooden prayer. The mind routed
with the heart, I could hardly move.
Then endless afterwards turned day,
and slow light blotted my crying out:
"Lord Nothing bring me back to love."

II.

Soon, love, you will come by air,
reverse journey of exiles and emigrants
who heaved their trails on waves
five miles below. No bones float there
of those who died, those jettisoned
from coffin ships of their American wakes.

The fish and history picked them clean,
though somehow mine lasted out the trip—
by remnant's luck no Elpenors,
though I'm part offspring of the sty;
American but dissatisfied
and orphan of my parents' heaviness.

You know all this who are yourself
en route and rootless, as I am.
To be neither one thing nor the other
is to be other always, our sad truth.
You are my one home in transit,
with me always never soon enough.

THE LIFT

He must be ninety if a day, and lives
one flight below us with his ancient wife
who looks a little younger—eighty-five?
Lazy mornings we meet them on the *lift*
after our late night up or late night out.
He squeezes in with his folded walker
and she follows, having taken his free arm
protectively, guiding him past the doors
that lurch shut behind them.

                      Elevator
we say where we're from, as though pulleys
were in the word, no choreography
of bodies—saints, angels, the deity—
bright ascensions into the empyrean.
How long has this pair been together?
Fifty, sixty, maybe seventy years,
having lived through most of the century
on this island drenched with rain and history.

Visitors here, we smile and make small talk
neighbors in name and only for a time,
a couple less than half their age and foreign,
knowing nothing of their lives except nods
and greetings, shared words in different use
like passing lives acknowledged and missed,
this slim room bearing us indifferently down.

BANSHEE

The long, drawn-out howling of a dog
shut up all night inside the auction ring
out back of our B&B scares awake
the owner's child so that she cries
in the room below our bed, a duet
that in my half-sleep seems to carry
beyond Mount Eagle and Slea Head
to my grandmother's Brooklyn apartment
thirty years ago where, back-lit in her chair,
she told me her story of the banshee,
how as a child she heard it wail
through the townland of Kilvendoney the day
the neighboring farmer died; and again
years later she listened to what sounded
like the keening of an old woman
under Sixth Avenue streetlights,
and knew then that no prayer could save
her oldest son lying in a coma,
meningitis working into his brain,
the pain like a small voice rising to a pitch
beyond all hearing—a noise so unlike
the steady hum and beep of machines
that monitored your induced sleep
in the outpatient wing where they carved
the lump from you, as it turned out,
benign, the word soothing as the whisper
this child's mother must use to calm
the fractured music in her daughter's throat,
Shush, shush, it's only an old watchdog,
as moonlight softens the tin roof
outside both our windows, and I draw you
closer to me in our rented bed
and rest my hand on your scarred breast.

INISHBOFFIN SUITE

I.

With our hired car behind us on the pier,
waiting forlornly like a pet for our return,
the ferry chugging from the narrow channel,
its diesel pungent on the soft day's air,
we felt ourselves ready for the open
of Cleggan Bay, mists on the slopes of hills,
two fishermen riding swells in a *curragh*
they'd jerry-rigged with an ancient outboard,
but not that whitecap traced on water's skin,
a flash, the dolphin's sudden plash and wink.

II.

Here's news for skeptics: scones and maps
of the island at the shop called "Shop."
At harbor's edge, Cromwell's ghost
still blusters from battlements falling shear
into flux, while on the rock below
the bishop he's tied there prays in Irish
to waves blunt as carved slate. Like corncrakes
sensing rain on wind, we could almost hear
the witch whose cast spell named this place,
her hard shriek, the White Cow lowing in stone.

III.

In Botticelli's *Spring* the shore's a commotion
of nymphs and Nereids, the goddess preening

for what would be the camera. In this harbor,
a beached trow churns; islanders pass silently
raising calloused hands, their faces weathered
as its hull. A moment ago, you walked outside
this lone café, and now you've returned,
your own face wind-burned, without make-up,
so it seems to shine. My heart swells. Our waitress
brings soup, brown bread, butter served on a shell.

IV.

That *pitch* spread beside the lapping strand,
its goalposts teetering like graveyard crosses,
might have been our gateway to fairyland
where we'd slept like Diarmuid and Grainne
among whispering dunes, the sky a soaked cloth
sprinkling us, the weariness of our bodies
holding us entirely to each other....
I dreamed of a swarm of bees chasing me
naked from the boghole, the acid lake,
you of the bruises flowering on your skin.

V.

All along the path, turfstacks piled
like cairns, the village diminished behind,
its whitewashed clay a mirror of peace
or desolation, the scree ahead a moonscape
of scat and wildflowers—vetch, knapweed,
bedstraw—the names you taught me. My mind

would be like this island, outcrop brooding
on its past, indifferent to news. But then
we were taking each new summit, fingering nettles,
crags of moss, gems of marble in the rock.

A DOLMEN IN THE BURREN

This raucous crew on a day trip from school
thinks it's a jungle gym they can climb on
and clamber up, until the quickest one
—sneakers scuffing stone—is king of a hill

that, once, was some real king's tomb: proud pile
engineered two, maybe three thousand years
before Archimedes perfected π,
the sign it preternaturally resembles

from this road in the middle of nowhere
growing, even now, more crowded with tourists
who hobble over ancient rundale walls
of a limestone landscape. Barren distances

find their center here, or seem to; a low sky
bleached the color of the ground bears down
nearly to the slab that might have been
a Mass Rock's tilting altar. Or is it a scale

lovers press their joined weights on, their bodies
rocking in equilibrium? So still
the couples come, after the itineraries
have called the bus-hordes further on, and build

from lesser stones these teetering monuments
in the larger's image. Remarkable how,
after how many years, no one's kicked them down.
They range like the remnants of a lost

city at the foot of its greatest vision,
some stone age Parthenon or Chartres
in whose every weathered fraction a world
assembles, for itself and for the lovers.

TWO BLACKOUTS

The Emigrant of Light—

Racine, Wisconsin

Even from atop the basement threshold
we could smell the ancient cylinder's burn.
And when we aimed the flashlight's beam we saw
the niche of must and cobwebs, its window
blackened like an ink stain from within.
All around us the neighbors' complaining buzz—
the chores undone, the TV shows missed.
But what of our own film lost at the credits,
our puzzled concern grown to frustration
as the lights dimmed, then dimmed more deeply,
nothing flooding the room with after-images?
We climbed back upstairs to slip from clothes
into a drawn bath, the mirrors misted,
candles melting our shadows to the wall.

Doolin, County Clare

The burden of our long drive behind us
west through midlands in blowing rain,
we walked in nightfall past upscale cafés
and new bungalows on a paved *boreen*,
our faces braced but freshened in the gale
that had roared in off the North Atlantic.
No rain now, only the wind's fierce absence
stalled us, or did we halt in amazement
at the townland blackened, no moon, no stars?
Two of a primal tribe, we followed on
with the others coming from distant fields

to the pub where someone reached for his fiddle,
as outside the cliffs fared into breakers,
and an old beacon wheeled its thin arm of light.

IN THE GREEN-WOOD

(Brooklyn, New York)

No country churchyard, where now the avenue
   blusters and throbs with weekend shoppers
hot for buys, its buses and delivery vans,
   cadenzas of boom-boxes and car horns,

but this archway like a cathedral wall
   fashioned out of brownstone, as though Upjohn
had turned to fresher labors, before steeple
   and vaulting nave and great rose window

found manifest form, so only this gate
   rises solitary above its city
of patient sleepers. Jet-lagged, nearly late
   for the tour, we pull up incongruously

it seems to us, as if we'd been sped back
   like Twain's time-shifter into stereoscope
only to discover the heart's true Gothic,
   a lost extravagance in our idea of home.

We fall in behind, following our guide
   through steam-blasted spires, the funeral bell
silent as our group rambles up the grade,
   our train boisterous, motley, raggle-taggle,

more Bruegel than Currier and Ives—
   those swallow-tailed, bonneted picnickers
on Sunday daytrips in their carriages,
   the graveyard less a graveyard than a park.

Here was heaven's waiting parlor, benign,
   tombs like villas along bluffs and dells,
ornate plots café-stocked with lounges,
   in unused fields the grazing animals

dissimulating into their fluent Eden.
    And here, still, is nature in pastoral,
little worse for wear, where Resurrection
    reclines like Autumn into the moraine.

Sylvan water, Crescent Water, Vision Path.
    Each floral lane and woodland boulevard
bends along the rim of a new expanse,
    weaves back again, a lost urban heaven

our guide unfolds in wit and anecdote:
    Colgates, Whitneys, Pierponts, the Steinways,
their grand mausoleum like an annex
    big enough to house a hundred guests;

Marcus Daley, Montana's "Copper King;"
    "Big Bonanza" Bill MacKaye, his crypt
heated like a marble country cottage
    for the grace of his eternal comfort;

Henry Ward Beecher, Horace Greeley;
    Basquiat, Bernstein, James Weldon Johnson;
Roosevelts, Morses, Tweeds, and Tiffanies.
    Though we prefer the less familiar stones:

Here lies Fannie, dog "with limpid eyes,"
    the sewing magnate's pet; brash Lola Montez
(a.k.a. Eliza Gilbert) who would drive
    men wild with her erotic "spider dance";

Macdonald Clarke, "Mad Poet of Broadway,"
    doggerel lines scrubbed from his obelisk;
Captain Hayes of the clipper ship *Rainbow,*
    these fathoms empty, his last voyage wrecked;

Bill the Butcher and Albert Anastasia,
    killers who called themselves "true Americans";
Do-Hum-Me, Barnum's Indian Princess,
    buried in her wedding dress, her husband

the brave weeping on her stone, like Azrael
    the angel of death; and the other lovers
with their iconographies of loss—
    a groom's pruned oak branch, a bride's clipped rose—

such early deaths. And here is a column
    transplanted under yews in this calm grove:
Matilda Tone, who buried her children
    and died alone. We'd seen her husband's grave

who slit his throat in the Dublin Barracks;
    saw his comrades in the vault at St. Michan's,
their bones crossed, skulls staring from their nests.
    For these doomed lovers, America was exile—

insufferable, "a culture of boors
    and swaggarts" she would suffer nonetheless,
her afterlife of life without him moored
    to a widow's dream of revolution.

And what if they had given up the cause,
    chose another life as settled farmers,
their heirs harkening to Greeley's "Go West"?
    Or would they become like Bellows' *Cliff Dwellers*

(the artist asleep in his unmarked grave)
    crowding sheer tenements? Now further on,
Battle Hill rises above the Narrows,
    Washington's stand, studded with monuments;

and other hills lush with Civil War dead,
    no masts in the harbor now, but barges
churning under the bridge for Gowanus docks
    astride the projects where my father lived;

and farther out, the island with its stalls
    and cages, its teeming, endless labyrinth
and line of faces, its railroad heading west;
    and farther west the meadowlands, and farther....

Here is the soul, a granite sphere with wings.
    Here pollen rains gold dust from the trees.
Monk parrots fruit the branches. We watch pass
    high sculpted clouds, opulent and migratory.

IX

TWENTIETH CENTURY
LIMITED

TWENTIETH CENTURY LIMITED

What is your friend's home port? How did he come?
Who were the sailors brought him here to Ithaka?
I doubt he came walking on the sea....

I. Wreck

My father's scuttled on the couch
watching the evening news
after a hard day at the docks,
his eyes fogged nearly shut, a sign
he's had a few on the way home.

No word passes between us
as we stare together at the tube
flickering its tale of a downed ship
vanished without a trace off Hatteras.
But now I hear his shoreman's voice

drown out the slick anchorman's:
"Have I told you the time
during the war a gunboat
exploded off the Admiralties?
It was the days before plastic bags.

"They had us fishing scraps of flesh
off the waves, then stuffing them
into burlap sacks for the families."
He nods his head towards the TV,
his face washed blue in the glow,

"But these poor bastards—they won't
find so much as a scrap in that sea."
It's the first we've talked all day,
and I'm grateful for even this story
I've heard it must be a hundred times.

"You were in Russia, too," I lead him,
"the snow was higher than your head."
But already he's sinking deeper
where he sits, and waves his hand
at me, "That's a thousand years ago,"

the words closing over on themselves.
I turn back to the news where the wreck
has given way to the weather
with its cartoon sun, a smiley face
peeling off a rain-hat for ray-bans.

My father starts like a watchman
in his perch: "I want to hear this."
I feel the line going slack
between us. Soon, he'll be splayed
face-down, adrift, asleep.

II. Twentieth Century Limited

This morning I woke already pacing in my sleep
Like a man whose wife has been in labor for hours
And still the child refuses to come, turned away
Inside the womb from the cradle of waiting arms

Until he's lifted from the breach, from the wreckage
Of his mother's body that, healed again, will sail on.
So for months I waited for the image of my father
Back from war. Then, in the half-light of a red sun

Disappearing into the Pacific, I stood like one
Of the great pitying angels in that German film I love

Who can do nothing but witness. How hard it is to pick
My father from the mass of sailors crowded at the rail

Of the destroyer easing into Navy Pier, headlands
Rearing above Point Loma and Mission Bay,
Their scrubby folds indifferent to the swell of figures
Waving banners, though there's no one to greet him.

And so I follow where he wanders through the city,
His mother dead, his father drowned in his bottle,
Or shivering DT's in his cell on Riker's Island.
In the hours before his train departs, he hits the bars

Along the harbor, in his seabag everything he owns:
The photograph he took of a Japanese soldier
Dead on Leyte Gulf, the Luger he picked up in Oman—
Souvenirs of the journey his sons would touch and love.

Now in the luminous smoke-haze I want to rest
My hand on his shoulder like an old pal from home,
To feel his thoughts pulse up my arm like a code,
Though little comes through—there are limits to angels:

Having his hair cropped with hedgeshears, diving off
The ship the way he'd dive off docks in Brooklyn,
How in the Admiralties he fished from oil-slick waves
The flesh of those torpedoed in the convoy....

His mother's face swims up, the image of his own,
The smell of apple butter in the boarding house
On Henry, running nickel beers at Kelly's Tavern.
Cat's Alley, Dollar Dye, the Gloria Theater,

Gray stones of St. Mary's Star of the Sea,
So different from this city's pristine mission walls.

121

The train station itself is a mission, as in the song
He used to hum about the swallows coming back.

In my father's head Goodman riffs his clarinet,
The diesel lurching east. La Mesa. Manzanita.
Names he can't pronounce, their music a piquant wind
Blown north of a border the sleeping continent ignores.

In the rocking Pullman I sit across from him, his image
In the window blending to the rewind of desert scrub
As the train fast forwards, his face morphing to the face
That surveyed the packed bar weekends at the Legion,

Stiff drinks and belly laughs with his fellow veterans,
Him tossing me quarters for the back room pool table.
Songs belted out to the tune of a player piano.
Wives in their bird's nest hats and fifties satin dresses,

Their kids fingering patterns in the shuffleboard dust,
Or outside in the scraggled hedges playing army.
Still the same crewcut, a badge of gray in the "V,"
He looks in control and vaguely discontented,

As though inside were a wound he couldn't name
But familiar to him, not like this painted emptiness,
Or the blanched distances he is unable to see—
Fired equations, the desert burned to a green glass.

Yet I'll find on his dresser that tie-clip—strange letters
Reading NAGASAKI buried in a jewelry case
Among his other links and pins. Is it in the seabag
Propped between his knees, the diesel swinging north

Toward the Great Divide? Having traveled so far east
He has come back west, only to press east again

Through what was once a sea of grass, sod dugouts
Of immigrants burrowed under the prairie's rim,

Their windmills whirring in the breakneck wind.
Gazing out at these cornfields, straight-edged roads
Running at right angles off the line, I can see
What my father cannot—in Red Cloud years ago

A girl sleeping with hot bricks in her bed, her eyes
A prairie sun drinking the land's iron solitude.
And now, striding along the primitive rich meadows,
Their unploughed innocence boundless and prodigal,

Afoot in this newer garden of creation, dense, joyous,
Modern, by all the world contributed, the burly Angel
Of these States, voluptuous, his embrace equal
To the smallest sprout, to the complete ensemble.

From the Rockies through the sandhills along the Plains
The Platte saunters toward its confluence, Missouri
And Mississippi widening slowly into the Gulf.
With little money, non-stop, my father rides this train,

Missing the juke-joints and blues bars of Kansas City,
St. Louis; missing the earthen temples—Monks Mound,
Cahokia, lost five hundred years in the American Bottom,
A farmstead cleared and raised atop the City of the Sun.

In Chicago I shadow him through Union Station,
The coin washroom where he baptizes himself home.
No time to see the skyscrapers risen from the fire,
Or catch the Dodgers on the road at Wrigley Field

Before the last leg, the Twentieth Century, roaring east
Through Indiana; roaring along Lake Erie's wasted shores,

Its canneries and shipyards where the homeless poet
Answered the Sirens with his true sublime.

Crossing the Ohio, the line rises over Appalachian hills,
Through blunted woodland peaks to the Water Gap.
Where the train veers into its final tunnel, my father
Stares in silence at the Empire State, its sword-hilt

Gleaming over the Meadowlands, over the tenements
Where he was born, the Navy Yard, the scatter of docks
He'll work for years. And already it's flooding
Into memory, the seabag folded in the hope chest,

The watch cap buried under wedding albums, bags
Of photographs, infants' clothes, until I'm standing
Before him, no angel now, or if an angel—Rilkean,
Terrible—the hurt son staring from across a continent

Who believes these years of distance are impassible,
His face sorrowed, too, as he puts his hand on my shoulder.
And my body electric in its woundedness saying,
"Do not touch me. I do not want to be touched."

III. Tattoo

Through each illness my father's raging cells
  retain the expression of this black pool,
blank swatch of ink his forearm brandishes
  like a birthmark or wound. I'm drawn to it
whenever I return to childhood's house,
  the tattoo floating in a fog of white hair
like some mottled raft crowded to the brink
  with swarms of faces, indistinguishable.

124

In my small hands I'd hold it to my own.
  And as I looked hard—his arm almost free
of its living weight—I'd make out a rose,
  and inside it a scroll, and inside that
a word: calligraphied *Mother* my father
  had burned into his body forever.

        ✍

My father burned into his body forever
  a boy's speechless pain. Seventeen, orphaned,
newly enlisted, he chose this icon,
  his right arm blooming to what now remains:
cipher, hieroglyph, smudge of a rune;
  a shadow of a leaf on wintry ground;
the mark, the brand, the palimpsest and blur
  of time's quoin printed on the flesh of time;
oil slick and galaxy, sunspot and rue;
  the dark god's torchlight and map of the grave;
bitter pond the lost sailor stares into,
  his mother's face flowering with the shades;
black hole, nebula, indelible scar;
  an eyelid's backward witness to its star.

        ✍

Missing sixty years, back like a shooting star,
  her image surfaced in a dead uncle's attic.
Disowned daughter of Southern wealth,
  she married a man doubly taboo: Irish
and Catholic, who maybe took this shot
  between bouts of drink and beatings. No sign
of my father's siblings. Youngest of ten,
  he's seven if a day, nestled in her arms
on a Red Hook roof. She'll die in seven years—
  her heart gave out at fifty-two. Small pet,

his puzzled face squints into some lost light
where I am standing now, where I can see
my own face in hers as his, in each a hint
of life eluding words, and love's imprint.

X

THE RING

NEAR HAG'S HEAD

(Cliffs of Moher, Ireland)

This headland is the battered prow
of a ship my silent father rides
into the Atlantic. Gust after gust
buffets the raw crag of his face,
his windbreaker flapping like a sail.

He could be his own father's grandfather
the way he stands before the rail
as others stood before the hold, the blind
journey before them, and nods to me
in recognition despite the ocean between us.

Even he knows on these cliffs the dead
are reading aloud from the book of the wind.

A CEMETERY IN BROOKLYN

Cast iron sky. A flock of gulls hover
like scavenger angels above the city,
blocks that are beehives of teeming cells.

And in this cemetery in Brooklyn
I search with my father down sidestreets
of stone-encrypted names for one

that bears our own. Among baroque houses
of the dead the humbler monuments
assemble, rows of dominoes studding

the half-frozen ranges named for saints.
Through line after line of graves we circle
in our impatient dance, checking numbers

against the map's xeroxed hieroglyph
until, at the wrought iron edge of the yard,
we find the modest stone, the grave

of my father's father, William,
forgotten fifty years, never visited.
When he died at the end of the Second War

he was fifty-eight and dissipated,
his own father's age at death
(*The Tobin men never make sixty,*

I heard my aunt say once in passing),
a spoiled mother's boy sent to Riker's,
the vicious drunk who beat his wife;

though, as legend has it, brilliant,
the one indispensable engineer
at the Navy Yard, battleship blueprints

clear in his head as the special detail
tracked him to Kelly's or Kilgallon's—
Wild Bill Tobin out of Red Hook,

poor immigrant's son who married
a daughter of Southern wealth disowned
for the transgression. Ten children

and none came to the funeral, but one,
the youngest, my father, just twenty
and back from war, the scar of a dog-bite

on his upper thigh, indelible
as a father's neglect, Odysseus's wound
suffered in the flesh of Telemachus.

I see it in his seventieth year,
my father having defied his fate:
the ghost-life of his speechless hurt,

its brutal charm, the smoky bars
and car-crashes of my childhood,
how he grows more solitary every year,

rehashing stories of his close calls—
convoys shelled crossing the Pacific,
the pier explosion at Luchenbach.

Now, once more he circles the stone
before turning back to the car,
his death wish his inheritance

and my own. I've felt it surge
under my skin, like this hard ground,
a coldness capable of anything—

though the mausoleums do their best
to seem Roman barques, or boats on a sea
where thousands tread water to keep afloat.

And someone takes it as their good work
to tend this obscure grave and others
with the patient duty of an unknown hand.

THE BOOK OF RUTH

Let her glean even among the sheaves, and do not reproach her....

In the beginning: everything *in medias res*.
And the past? Most of it dark matter
winnowed from diminished stars, an absence
necessary, the sustaining emptiness....
Like this book I've never read, it having been
withdrawn, a kind of family holy grail,
the diary kept by my father's mother, Ruth,
in which the names of the generations
are preserved for as far back as she knew,
its not-there-ness its legend and colophon.

So I choose a beginning, *in medias res* myself.
Say 1908. The twenty-year-old bride
in love with generations jots her book
of names in a Red Hook tenement, a history
branching back, the dark matter, each present
absent as a star erased from sight. In two years,
her sisters will be dead, in four her brother,
and she already disowned—her exile
her mother's rage at her lover's offense.
"Tonight he winnows barley at the threshing floor."

It's a kind of holy grail, her mother's birth
in Richmond, 1861, colophoned in the diary:
Julia Meade Dotson, her life a legend
salvaged from the emptiness, then withdrawn.
As far back as she knew is farther still,
though her father, George, built breakwaters,
lighthouses—history books witness this—
before Manassas, Gettysburg, The Wilderness,
now all of them names among the generations,
her own mother an erasure, a diminished star.

Ruth is winnowing what she can, gleaning
life from poverty on Henry Street, her children
ten small stars in the dark matter of generations,
her husband withdrawn into alcohol. A son
of emigrant Irish who emptied from coffin ships
in medias res for a new beginning,
he thrashes her till she wishes herself nameless;
she who came softly, banished by her mother,
as though she had given up her native land
for life in a Brooklyn tenement, her holy grail.

Ruth is withdrawing to a house in dark matter,
emigrating to absence without light, without
beginning, and holding her children's hands
who were begotten of William—"tonight he winnows
barley at the threshing floor." In her book,
all the names appear in memory's colophon,
the heart's holy grail, the mind's sustenance,
and what she knew we know, as though her sight
had been blended with our own *in medias res*,
father, mother, and the erased generations.

If I could scroll back into the past, banished
as I am *in medias res*, emptied of beginnings,
I would winnow a sustenance greater than names:
Ruth and Julia, George, Neddy and David.
Diminished stars. Each life a life that mattered
in the darkness, the unaccountable there-ness
that surpasses legend—George Gordon Meade,
his holy grail preserving the Union
and a modest fame, Gettysburg's savior, Grant's
subordinate, his life now a life in colophon.

Withdrawn by history, her book diminishes
into dark matter, the chronicle of names
never to be read in the living colophon

of her hand, that holy grail, that absence
toward which the soul tacks, an obsessed sailor
in quest of home, his desire a fugue, a flight
from the beginning to the beginning
in medias res, all around him emptiness,
mother dead, father dead, with the generations,
and everything not there sustained by legend.

Come softly banished legend, daughter Ruth,
in medias res as in the beginning,
mother in dark matter whose name is pity,
out from history and its endless winnowing,
bridal Ruth, bookish Ruth, mother of generations
and your ten diminished stars—James and William,
Catherine, Ruth, Edward, Edna, Frank, Helen,
Alan, and Gerard, the youngest, my father
also gleaned, a grail, not here, not anywhere.
And this too shall be preserved in the emptiness.

502 SCHENCK AVENUE

(Brooklyn, New York)

Not there, I should have guessed, the tenement
where I found they had lived a century
ago, the gone, the ghosts in the gene pool
swimming face down in the tide of the soul,
the great-greats, the errant progenitors.

They are an air that has been forgotten.
They are a signal flashed from the Distant
where the offing grays to the wing of a gull
                that is not there.

And now these strangers, newer immigrants
time-bound as my own, the old buildings burnt
in rage, in riots years ago, or felled
in the windfall of some false renewal:
They will go like nomads from numbered tents
                into what's not there.

THE DOCK ROAD

(Liverpool, England—for Michael Palma and Joseph Lennon)

... e poi che mosso fue,
in trai perlo cammino alto e silvestro...

Nearing the end we left the workhouse site,
    the old wall crumbled like bread over ground
    when, turning to the group, our learned guide
continued ruefully: "The Great Hunger,
    An Gorta Mor, drove thousands to stations
    along this route, millions from the ruin
their world had become. Through that iron gate
    at Clarence Dock the poorest of the poor
    crowded without relief, into *Straid Lace*
glutting tenements, burning with fever,
    starving where they still could speak their own tongue,
    or drifting like dead souls to the river
where they loaded into ships—as if Charon
    were a ferryman fording the Mersey—
    then off they sailed in their floating coffins.
Some of you may think such allusions fancy,
    but in Dante the damned *are* historical,
    though I'm not poet enough to rhyme *Mersey*
with *Mercy*—there was little. Ironical
    to hear nuance in such words: *Mourne* and *mourn*
    for instance—the granite memorial
cut from those mountains like a standing stone
    for the suffering hammered into dust,
    and the grief that passes understanding.
It almost appears they never did exist,
    except we are here, unlikely as the saved,
    though something smarts of guilt in our witness.
This city mortared with the blood of slaves
    manufactured wealth for old world and new
    on the backs of the oppressed. Every race
walked the dock road, or nearly: Irish and Jew,

Chinese, African, German, Italian;
    though to say *race* is wrong: there is one queue
only, and we're all in it until it ends.
    Which, my friends, brings us here, to this car park
    off Hope Street. If you're struck by the absence
of all but the habitual you're right
    in your judgment, though this was a mass grave.
    Maybe you can imagine them rising,
the historically damned, ghosts in heatwaves
    off tarmac, though they are migrant even
    from this home. Life, my friends, is progressive.
Two thousand paupers, exiled by famine,
    were buried here, you can see by the plaque
    embossed obscurely against the new dorm,
like a coin of the divine economy,
    or at least the coffers of the local.
    Wherever they are now they won't be back.
You might look for them under your boot soles,
    as your Whitman wrote, and on that I'll end
    my tour." He walked away like an exile
himself, but a soul at ease in his skin
    of the remnant. A high, late morning sun
    struck the windshields blindingly, a gash
of light, migrainous, cutting as ice
    along the glass. Some murmured about lunch,
    while others of us stood a time in silence.
And I followed down that path of weeping shades.

CROSSINGS

A riff on Stevens' "Our Stars Come From Ireland"

What would the water have been
without these indelible stains—
slaves heaving dead slaves overboard
while the ship cleaves its cargo to port;

and north of that middle course
this other, likewise riding west:
refugees, brutalized, abandoned,
bones gnawed by the dogs of famine?

Each changes the habit of mind
out of its distance, unheard,
until what's made returns to emend
what it is, and its origins.

The sea from its luminous east
churns in the length of its chains.
This ocean bears more than stars
on the cold aesthetics of the waves.

ST. JOHN

St Mary's (Cemetery) is located at the crest of a windswept knoll,
on the south side of Loch Lommond Road, in East Saint-John.
There are no markers or fences to define its actual parameters...

        On these shores
the ocean slides like a veil from the continent,
        rocking tides from half a world away
    withdraw
            in a froth of seething dulse
where the bay's laid bare to slosh and wrackline.
                Terns print momentary Braille
on the sea-bed shiny as shellac, and cast-up
            islands appear lost Atlantises
            outlasting
                the incredulity of the stunned explorer,
or whale-backs for some new Brendan to mistake
        before his quest resumes.
    On these shores
the old city, hasped by modern bridges, stares
        at itself across a river flowing
    in reverse
                against the Fundy as though against
            itself—scale after scale of whirlpools—
    and years of tourists
marveling at the gorge. Cruise ships
        glide sleek hulls into the harbor,
moor at quays
        along Water Street, the crowds
emptying into shops on Prince William, St. Germaine,
        gentrified gargoyles
            hovering like geniuses
over steam-blasted facades of the vanished wards.
            On these shores
    time swirls
backwards in a dream of race memory. The shipyards
                brim with "shovel-fisted Irish,"

rag-heaped slovens wheeled by the remnant
  of gutted townlands.
 They gather
outside the waterfront's slop-bucket tenements
  —Flagor's Alley, York Point—
King's Ward, Duke's Ward, Sydney Ward, Portland;
 riot through the cholera-strafed streets
   against Loyalist bunting and Orange drums.
 On these shores
ghosts speak the lingo of lost tongues and shipwrights,
 of keel and keelson,
   of reamer, hauser, fid, and maul,
dead-strap, dead-eye, straker, oakum, sawpit.
   On these shores
the scribers notched their signatures in timber
 Brayons axed in the Micmac forests
  for Cunard to fill with conifer and trade,
to return again with their starving human ballast.
  The Alms House
 purveyed its "fine healthy children,
  bound out
to proper persons on immediate application"—
  orphan charges
 discharged like slaves at auction.
 On these shores
the Guatemalan restauranteur adorns his shop-front
 with rainbow displays of home.
Trees canopy the Loyalist Burial Ground
   in century's-old growth,
 while the immigrant cemetery beside the refinery
  rots in its shower of acid rain.
 On these shores
the *ceilidh* still thunders on late into the night
 in backroom pubs
  where the latest heirs
of history recede into their undreamt futures.

Lovers make love
    in trashed gun-emplacements,
and the new Museum rises astride the new Hilton.
      But on these shores
there is no sea-road to that island off the coast
    with its quarantine stations
  and graveyards
where coffin ships emptied their wasted holds
      —*Aeolus* and *Swan*—
    the light-bearing names;
and salt winds off the Great Banks lick the Cross
  raised in remembrance,
    while the lighthouse signals its golden door
      to an offing
that levies its apocalypse of fog over the town
  from High Point to the breakwaters.
      On these shores
where tombstones recede into earth like shells
    below the tide,
I riffle through remains of dig books
        to find my own past,
then drive with my love to the bare knoll's crest,
    the stone gateposts gateless,
  no walls, no boundary,
and walk among the footstones, lost avenues,
    currents of grass, still ponds
  of moss
      fast rising to erase the names.
  On these shores
I kneel inside the empty townland of the dead
    for James and the others,
      travelers
who left no trace but this code in my bones,
  an unmarked grave, the tern's trail
    of history,
and the tide coming in with a screech of seabirds
    on these shores.

THE RING

I followed the winding coast road back
from Cobh, Annie Moore and her brother
cast in bronze at the Center entrance
who were head of the line at Ellis Island,
now looking as though they inquired directions
in their own country; inside, the dim passage
through American wake and coffin ship,
the clutched figures of a prior generation
reeling to swells and sound-effects, each hold
frozen in the ache of crossing; further on,
the surprise exhibit with my father's ship,
United States, steaming into the harbor
the way it steamed into the Narrows
below the rising towers of the bridge.
Above the quays, St. Colman's presided
over the dock where my mother's mother
waited for the tender, where my father's
forefather, lost in the crush, disappeared
under the raw deck of the lumber boat,
human ballast teeming like vermin
on bodies in the fields they fled at home.

"I can tell you where the Tobins first landed,"
my welcoming host remarked, then invited me
to the canopied patio beside the house,
chinked glasses of whiskey neat and golden,
the garden luminous in the long twilight.
"If you drive east beyond Killeagh and Youghal
on the way to Dungarvan, off to the right
you'll come on the Ring Road, *Rinn na nGael*.
There are Tobins there still from Norman times:
St. Aubyn, Toibin, the name gaelicized,
then anglicized into your own name now."
I had known the history but not the place.
So next day driving along the proffered route
each village seemed a station on a journey

of return. Kinsalebeg, Grange, Keily's Cross....
I had pursued the paper trail, unwound
the brede of names through census and baptism,
each generation rechristening the last,
until custom faltered like a language
on the tongue, until the trail trailed off
into the mists of the unrecorded.
Now, I was tracing a highway to origin,
the road unreeling that was once *boreen*
through townlands where the starving wandered,
their potatoes scorched black with blight
as though a fire had rained over them;
grubbers of nettles, weeds, their faces
swollen with fever, stench of *bloody flux*
rising from *scalps* where the evicted burrowed.
"Men like famished dogs scoured the fields,"
an official wrote. "I saw in one cottage
a roil of rats feasting on an infant.
Nowhere have I witnessed anything like it,
not in Calcutta, not in Dahomey—
the voiceless children silenced by hunger,
whole towns turned to habitations of ashpits,
the bodies burned at night, leaving no trace."

Descending the Drum Hills, beyond Gorteen,
I turned off the main road following signs
in a language I had lost before I was born.
This was *gaeltacht*, remnant of the Deise,
land before the land was renamed and hushed.
What was left for me, generations gone?
A perfume of turfsmoke fresh in my nostrils:
pasture's green reach to the head and the bay;
thick fuchsia hedges; roads that were cowpaths
where locals greeted with slowly raised hands,
or a nod of the cap to my stranger's car:
the postcard my eye had framed in its longing.

144

Then, Mooney's Pub, where I stopped for a pint
and let slip my quest. "So you're a Tobin,"
Aine said, accommodating my English.
"They're all about here. Have you heard of Nioclas,
the great singer?" She showed the photograph
with its dark hair and features, unlike my own,
though a vague resemblance to a dead uncle,
but I couldn't say for sure. What was The Ring
but another station, happened on by chance
or seeming grace? So why not trace further
through lost Norman crests, or track DNA
to nomadic tribes six thousand years gone
from the banks of the Ganges; or further back
through each human cell to African Eve,
her grunts our shibboleth tuning savannahs?

I felt the gift, shared thrumming in the bones,
later that night in the crowded room
when all the instruments had gone silent
and a man rose up shyly, regally alone,
and sang *sean nos* one of the singer's songs:
It's a beautiful country I take you to
by the blackwater streams of the Deise,
where the thrush and the blackbird sing sweetly
and the wild deer range over the mountains,
where branches bend low with fruits and blossoms
and all the hives brim over with honey,
where the cuckoo croons the whole summer long
and the corncrake lifts its cries in the grass.

XI

THE RAINBOW CAFE

THE RAINBOW CAFÉ

I.

This August's moon's a ballroom globe
stilled above flustered banners of clouds
whose outlines shift with each soft gust
outside my childhood window.
Below, the scraggled rowhouse yards
appear content to breathe what's left
of the long day's humidity and exhaust
while sirens bend away for blocks
and someone revs his engine down the street,
and the air's electric with borrowed light.
It's nights like these, my parents asleep,
I'd forage through the hope chest, albums
nested deep in cedar, pictures of their life
before I was born, like movie stills:
my mother flowing in her satin gown
down the aisle where my father waits,
"Highpockets Tobin" lost in his tux,
but not nervous, his face aglow,
the priest blessing them with lifted arms,
them kissing like I never saw them since.
Then both families off to The Rainbow
Café, the band playing Dorsey
as my father whirls my mother
under the spinning globe, splinters
of light glinting off their faces,
everyone applauding then joining in
with my parents who are dancing
and refuse to stop, their young bodies
moving each with a life of its own
closer to the other, each shining
like the globe itself, shining together
in their first night's pleasure.

II.

I remember mawkish Forties flicks
where lovers embrace in shades
of black and white. They gaze
passionately across the gulf
of their separateness, the audience
knowing their solitudes will be bridged
(How they want them to be bridged),
though the words can't be believed,
eyes moving mouth to eyes, eyes
to mouth *I love you, I've always
loved you*, each actor's lips
pressed unopened to the other's—
and picture how my parents met
at Fort Hamilton's USO, my father
in crew-cut and uniform, survivor
of Africa, Leyte Gulf; my mother
made up like a flapper, so far
from the nun she thought she'd be.
He moves through the music hall,
soldiers, sailors, would-be brides,
she sees him and she knows—
James Stewart and Donna Reed
in *It's a Wonderful Life.*
Though they're more like Fred
and Ginger when they dance,
the way they do at The Rainbow Café
three years later—Foxtrot,
Two-Step, Jitterbug, Lindy....
And what of that other dance
I remember: the three of us
in their shattered bed, me
in the middle hoping to quiet
killing words fired across the gulf

that had grown between them,
stunned hush when they fell asleep,
the streetlight's globe buzzing
through the window, pouring over us
its brute and barren glow?

III.

Memory, too, is a ballroom, the dancers
returning as I do these summers
I come home. When I leaf through albums,
their life assembles, captive fragments,
poses struck for the camera, each one
vivid as a rainbow, its colors shading
into the next, as though the globe
could spin back in perfect nostalgia—
the way my parents danced together
at family weddings, movements silken,
even the bride and groom receding
to marvel at them, perfect energy
wedded to perfect grace, my father
in his sixties twirling my mother
as though she were a girl, her free hand
thrown back, O pure art that says here
is the actual, their eyes holding each other
as though no one else was there.

IV.

So this is paradise: slide-step,
dip and turn, your partner

a motion that follows your lead
until you are the one motion,
no one to lead or follow,
having become the music
to which your bodies give
visible form, the floor
forgotten like the earth....
In The Rainbow Café
it's October 2nd, 1948,
and my parents dance away
the middle of the century,
time a globe they sway inside,
dance that marries them
to all the other dancers.
My mother's parents shuffle
along the floor, exiles
from an older world,
while my father's spin
with the other dead
among the slow waltz of stars.
And louder now, at the edge
of the hall: a percussion
of guns, the blood-drunk
dance of armies, men
my father joined at war;
and now the dance of flesh
sizzling, of ashes whirled
from the horrible barracks,
so high even God stops
dead in his heaven
as my parents dance on and on.

V.

The moon's not a globe to mirror innocence,
symbol of the mind's untrammeled sight.
It is the flashlight of a camp guard
aimed at the cowering. Or it is
what it is—radiant ball of dust
we calculate and shuttle to, imaginable
as my own belated bus-ride
to The Rainbow Café, its boarded windows
desolate as pictures the dead keep
to remind themselves of the living.
For nearly fifty years my parents
danced their solitudes, dance of fist
on table, crippled dance of silence
as they sat in their matching chairs.
And for nearly forty I've wondered
how they managed to keep going, my mother
barely able to climb upstairs, my father
taking my arm as we walk to his favorite bar.
In a museum, once, I saw figures on a door—
Adam and Eve's gawky dance as they staggered
through Eden, children taking first steps;
and God, the good Parent encouraging them,
the Dance-Master who sets the world
in motion, Director who pens his own script
until it comes alive in a flicker of light.
It could be them, asleep now, lying in bed
like old friends hobbling toward each other,
lovers, apart for years, marred by war.
And still here they are, palms held out
to make sure the other is real, almost touching.

DRINKING WITH MY FATHER AT MUSE'S BAR

Butcher, green grocer, luncheonette, altar rail,
once a week bingo at the Young at Heart,
coffee at Pegasus, The Green Tea Room;
then it's off to the garage to warm up the car
he can't drive anymore. But everyday
my widowed father's rounds end at Muse's
where he settles in, one of the regulars,
giving the sign for his afternoon drink.

This could be any dim watering hole
glimpsed into walking past, but this is here.
No need to order since everyone knows
what everyone wants, and everyone is named
but me—Turk the Tender, John the Bookie,
Big Fat Roger who bounces on weekends,
Jameson Jimmy, José the Gambler,
Killer Bill, Budweiser Bill, Bill the Suit.

And bellied up beside them: my father,
Dewar's Jerry, life-long exile to haunts
like this, where he would come into his own
outside his family's overweening eyes.
Connolly's, Spiro's, Hannigan's—now all gone.
Hours-long chin-fests, palaver thick as smoke
that drifted from my mother's cigarette
where she brooded alone in our kitchen.

Time moves in closed circuits of memory,
pools in the half-light of the TV's glow
where the horses rehearse each coming race
in races run before, an endless replay
like my father's story the day he found
my mother dead in bed beside him, or those
he told for months after, his life with her
unreeled into after-lives at one remove.

I nurse my beer and listen to the talk
of Aqueduct, Belmont, the betting pools—
such ease, as if a life without regrets
blessed each of these cronies, my father, me.
And soon, surprised, I find myself at rest
among this motley crew, sharing their jibes
till Turk says, "Hey Jerry, your son's alright."
"Yeh, I know—he's a first class ballbuster."

Outside the bar he takes my arm, unsteady,
as we walk to the same apartment house
he's lived in fifty years. "I'm glad you're home,"
and "I miss your mother." Then, up the stairs:
"I need to rest—go on ahead of me."
I make my way myself up the last flight
while he sits beside the landing window,
his blunt face shining in the low evening light.

GALILEE

(A seaport town in Rhode Island)

Now that my father's dead, I've come again
To Galilee, combing inside the little shops
For some trace of him among the knick-knacks
He loved to browse: silver-dollar corals,
Conch shells, chintzy boats-in-bottles,
Driftwood, "the moon's" brightly polished stones

Swept up by waves, dipped in shellac.
It's March, off-season, the sun
A pale coin burnt on the horizon's
Wash of cloud. I pace the Beach Road
Past shingled inns, their windows boarded
For squalls, hoping to glimpse his back

Among the dunes—the way I did that summer
Years ago, just out of college, already lost.
We hardly spoke. I'd witnessed the cost
Of disappointment on his face: inhewn lines
Webbing his cheeks and brow, bulging temple-veins.
A brief, weekend escape from the grind. He looked older,

His shoulders sloping where he stared into the sea,
My mother beside him, ankle-deep in blowing sand—
A lost tribe's totems blinded by wind,
So frail the slightest gust could topple them.
He waved me over. Against the tattered scrim
Of Point Judith, we watched as the packed ferry

Shoaled towards the pier, tourists back from the Vineyard
Gathered for shore. He wanted to take that boat
The next day, but didn't. His reticence was rote—
Rarely risking the least unseen prospect
For the promise of some larger contentment:
"I've always rolled with the punches." One day his heart

Stopped. For months I wondered what his mind
Held in that moment. Was it knife-thrust
Or the cold diffusion of this sea? What faces
Shattered there? So much I didn't know
Of him, so much of me I closeted in shadow.
I still feel my mother's nails clawed into my hand.

In Galilee now, I watch as the winter ferry heaves
Into the Sound, only a few perched at the rails,
Braving the marbled water. Through clouds, the failed
Sun whitens deeper into the gathered mist.
Scraps like ash wash in with the tide. I wait
For what light there is to walk towards me on the waves.

MY MOTHER'S EYE

She kept it in its plastic case beside
her carousel of pills, the single contact
she wore in place of the left lens she lost
from a blown cataract. "I have to put
my eye in," she'd say, unscrewing the cap,
then would fish with her fingertip to find
that clear horizon submerged in its well,
a bubble she'd balance in the kitchen air.
She always winced inserting it, then clasped
her hands to her face as though it pained her
more than it possibly could. Before bed
it was the same, the ritual reversed,
my father stretched in his plastic-wrapped chair
watching the last of the ten o'clock news.
For twenty years I gauged her slow decline
when I'd come home, able to do nothing,
until with every visit I could trace
the lineaments of a greater distance
in the way she looked, the bride hollowed
from her glowing pose, her going under
a lone swimmer's turn away from shore.

Impossible to say what hurt her so—
something burgeoning blandly in the pool
of her diminished past, some childhood blame
for a brother's death, self-placed, or forged
out of her parents' grief, though chance whispered
the virus into his ear, into his brain.
Or maybe it was the loss of a life
she'd planned without this husband, these sons.
One late night in the kitchen's haze, her eyes
glazed over, her face wracked with drink, I saw
the unhealed glare of her long resentment:
"I always worked, two jobs when Pop got sick.
I'd just started college—all incompletes."
Her fingers squeezed a cigarette's slow burn.

"I worked nights at Woolworth's. He got sicker,
and it was pointless. Then I met your father...."
"You could still go back," I heard myself say,
"Night School." But she was shaking her head,
flesh starved to bones under her nightgown
as she poured another glass. "My life is over."
So she thinned, the Sibyl of her own myth,
for years prophesying her imminent end.

And after it was fulfilled, I walked
through the kitchen as my father slept
alone in their bed, still stunned by her stare
that last morning when he woke beside her,
the anti-depressants she refused to take
snug in their bottles on her carousel.
A stubbed-out cigarette, her lipstick printing
its filter-less rim, lay in her ashtray.
And there, on the bright floral tablecloth,
her lens-case sat, and inside—her eye
suspended in solution, floating like a cell
in the womb of its familiar waters,
unscathed, dreaming itself, waiting to grow.

ELEGY

Where does it come from now—disturbance
of the air, your voice a breath of wind,
muffled hum strained for through years like gauze,
or sound waves caught in skull's resonant bone?

My voice or yours? If yours, barely audible,
still it breaches the passage, thrums inside,
takes its shape at the ear's forge and hurtles
for the curled shell of sound, for the labyrinth:

Once you had a brother, that child at prayer
in the old print you kept on your dresser,
forever posed in his first communion suit,
black hair combed back, his face so like yours

he could be my brother, his hands a church,
folded temple from which rosaries hung
their given cross. You held those small hands
on walks to the park or crossing the street.

What you could not see was the bone's process,
the knot of poison in the honeycomb
where temporal plate meets cartilage,
and his absent future like a depth-sounding

through fathoms of your life, incessant tune
played and played again in some dark chamber.
Did you blame yourself? Did I become him,
crammed in the carriage, belated infancy?—

how you'd wait up nights for your grown son
I thought you were killed to return home,
though I had moved away, had turned away
from hands that would hold me tight as bottles

hidden under chairs, or that raw crucifix
you'd press into your palm to make the wound
palpable, to make your body the host
of the speechless thing that consumed you.

After you died, I found the police blotter
among the safe deposit scraps, your fingerprints
the ham-fisted stain of your father's punishment
for running away—were you ten years old?—

unable to stand the loss. Then the weeks
kept from home at relatives, then the years
with their refusals and failures of love,
with their trials of forgiveness falling deaf.

I hear what I can never know of your pain
like imagined rumblings from that fenced in lot
where you said they'd kept the ape Gargantua,
its huge form stalking through the wilderness.

Mother, that name you never taught me
to call you, that echoed like embarrassment,
what frequency will carry it to you now
who are less than a whisper, a hiss of tides,

this amplitude, this silent drumming in my ears?

AFTERLIVES

I. *The Mirror*

Its backing brittle as ancient parchment
  that crumbles in my hand as I lift it
from the wall, the hooked wire gripping
  the mount where it hung for fifty years
as my parents moved in, then out of its space
  mornings they readied for work; or lingered
weekday evenings, worn out, watching shows
  on the television's chattering square,
while my brother and I piled on the couch
  or, bored, rough-housed around the place,
our father threatening *I'll get the strap—*
  all of us unaware of our reflections,
as though we were actors on this larger screen
  where, now they're gone, the empty room
tilts, then slides past into its crate. Old night.
  And a char of quicksilver conjuring light.

II. *The Rings*

  One has a plastic statue
chained to its tarnished orbit,
   right arm raised with a torch
    that glows, the apex
     of kitsch.

  One has a heart and a hinge
that swings to a pointing man
   whose curtained chest parts open
    to a flaming heart
     and crown.

162

Others have names of countries
on leather embossed or inked,
    Caribbean Island cruises
        far away from doors
            the keys

    would click wide year after year
revealing familiar rooms—
    the same keys you slip off now
        from the rings that slide
            like zeros,

        one by one
    from everything gone.

XII

OUTERBRIDGE CROSSING

OUTERBRIDGE CROSSING

For me the commonplace deserves to be praised since
history's volcanic malice rages beneath the thin
layer we tread so carefully....

As though airborne in our brief skins we follow
the rise of the ramp with other cars rivering
over the river's end of the Narrows,

the Verrazano a huge graded bow, a crest
we ride with all the rest, everyone a world
in a cruising bubble, blood-cells streaming west

through each tower's outsized needle's eye,
on either side a prospect—the vaulted city
a bed of crystals slowly accruing sky;

and out beyond the other flashing rail
Gravesend Bay churning into its offing,
each slow wake dispersing like the vapor-trail

of a jet you can barely make out in the blue,
or like memory's trace when the moment passes
and it moves ahead and what moves ahead is you.

     ℒ

The flip-up seat of my parents' Rambler wagon....
The *way-back* I called it, after the time machine
on that cartoon I loved with its near-sighted dog

and boy side-kick bounding back centuries
for confabs with Plato, Shakespeare, Napoleon,
his lever's flick rectifying history.

The way-back is where I'd ride those weekends
our family would escape to the country
in that car with its monster grill and angel wings

flying over the Narrows along the new bridge,
its skyway grounded where the Ambrose lightship
guided boatloads. Gone the lightship, the ferry

that bore our numbered heads across the harbor
before it rose, emblem of the mundane sublime,
between two forts above the emptying river.

Gone now those numbered heads—father, mother—
and my own face in the wayback turning back
to find our house among the rows of huddled homes;

ahead lay the dead-end exit beyond Todt Hill
where the freeway stopped and my father turned
for the boulevard that led past Mount Loretto

with its tapered steeple, big as the cathedral's
in that picture book I'd pore over in school,
rising over sewer-less Tottenville

and the waste-fields near the Kill Van Kull
where they'd build the new cemetery, a ridge
of the great dump visible like an alp

from this outland passage and its orphanage.
So we drove to city's end, then over the Kill
to the final crossing. To the Outerbridge.

       ℞

Resurrection. Outpost of the dead. No high walls,
wrought iron rails; no gothic brownstone gates
lifted like a pair of folded hands; no vaults

where the well-appointed sleep in attitudes
of their earthly glory—monuments eroding
in rain, statuary angels, that Jazz great's

golden horn at rest on the crown of its stone.
No hills, no luminist maze of trees and glens.
Here, the storm fence measures numbered rows,

graves laid out like tract homes on flat ground
that my numbed father hardly manages to walk,
holding onto my arm as he stumbles to plywood

laid over grass and carpeted with plastic turf,
the casket propped on boards above its hole.
Mourners file behind. The priest recites his prayer

while the ritual director hands us each a rose
to lay across the lid. Rose of Longing.
Rose of Refusals. Rose of Dumbfounded Hope

that breaks in my father's hand. *Is it an omen?*
No, take mine. And then—what else to say
when saying falters?—*I'll be coming soon.*

As though in her box my mother were Penelope
each night unweaving her fate like the dress
that crowd below will clamor to strip clean.

ℒ

Back to Pearl Court then, the Christmas Eve
she knelt beside the sofa unwrapping gifts
and my father laid the last box at her feet—

shock and then tears when she saw the stole
in its nest of tissue, and the whole family
ran hands along her fur-draped shoulders,

a gift never wanted because never imagined,
for the time being her lost daughter forgotten,
and everything in all our small world was now.

&

Clockwise or counter-clockwise? How my father
spun the car one winter Sunday coming home
from the country, the toll plaza's tarmac

a slick rink, windows a carnival midway
of whirling lights and horns, those screaming
riders ourselves under gas-jets flaming

like torches above refineries, the air
a crisp spume smoky as the atmosphere
inside the tavern we'd driven from, or

my grandmother's kitchen late afternoons
in Pearl Court, its palaver and card games,
its laughing clatches of kin and muted angers.

I wonder how he righted the car, how we ever
made it back that day across the Outerbridge,
unscathed and shaken; how we'd been furthered

by being errant, even our forgetting a motion,
slipping imprint left in the tire's wake,
our past ahead of us in the mirror's vision....

&

Or our future behind, what we were a summons
gnawing at the bones, until I made the journey
to fog-bound Saint John, that wasted cemetery

beside the refinery that, once, was spruce-line
declining to the Bay where terns and razorbills
still glide, freewheeling in their tangent heaven.

Below, stones crumble like sugar in poisoned air.
I moved among them, a dissimulation of one
tracing the dead's lost avenues, slabs fractured,

earth boiling up to fill the names, and me prone,
running my finger along the soluble letters
to mark the neighborhood of the unmarked grave

of James, Famine-son, my uncle's namesake, sailor
of the coffin ship that brought him here, exile
and remnant, "laborer of this city," old father

buried with others buried: Mary and Gertrude,
Arthur and Ellen, daughters and grandchildren,
all moss and scrub-grass like the rest—the dead's

immigrant townland testament to their poverty,
broken stones piled, the trees choked or dying,
those lives diminished out of lives into lives.

I thought of them as I drove back over the bridge
where the Saint John rolls into Fundy's tideways
and reverses itself, halted by the rocking bay

into eddies, whirlpools, a back-flowing falls,
as if the current were bent on refusing its end,
the river redoubled as if longing for its source.

171

∅

Among the wrack of Pearl Court's decimated rooms,
buried in the after-life of what's left behind,
I pulled it like a cache from the hope chest's tomb—

that old-time camera, its flash-arm a kind of horn
jutting from the cyclops' face, its inward eye
a shallow cave swept clean with each blink, the blank

slate of the moment at once forged and surpassed
in the shutter's click; left inside: a last reel,
along its row of portals the horizon of the past.

I rewound it carefully as an ancient scroll.
Though when it came back to me, it was as though
I looked ahead and not behind, each shot a window

where the blurred ghost-cruise sails into port,
and one where two figures stand close beside the bow,
dead mother, dead father—sunspot, penumbra.

∅

Now in Resurrection their names are carved in stone
as if stone itself were not slowly lifting off
into dark energy, or whatever motion

wheels the nano-second of each life inside its course;
for Gregory of Nyssa a forwarding and return,
apokatatasis, the soul's volta back

into the uncreated, our true home a furtherance—
flash of movement in stillness when a train
leaves its station, the hub's perfection

in the rim, each slipstream a fractal interval
of some infinite tide. And so my mother's body
in bed beside my father spins on in its fetal

somersault; and my father's floats on his trim
of sheets, like the sleeping sailor who dreams
of home until home is the dream that stays him

from its shore; or until they are assumed
as in that photograph where they're dancing
inside the Dublin gardens the year before her death,

mugging for the camera, spurred by the name
Disco Rose to make their bodies into figures
of light the shutter limned so they could dance on.

Here, in the shadow of the Outerbridge,
I almost feel names lifting from these stones
like particles of light somewhere becoming waves;

though we'll drive back, love, over the Narrows
into our own lives, our unborn still asleep
in the womb of our choice, and Gravesend

below, lustral in its self-emptying,
as though it rode a current deeper than history,
the sky bodied in its waters, bright and ongoing.

NOTES

In Lieu of a Preface

"One must start from home," John Montague writes in his preface to *The Rough Field*, "so the poem begins where I began." Unfamiliar to most American readers, Montague's classic long sequence about his ancestral townland in County Antrim, Northern Ireland affirms a profound connection to place, however fraught and wounded that connection might be. At the same time, the poem bears witness to the passing of a world. Unlike Montague's Garvaghey, the Narrows I grew up beside with its ships passing in and out of the harbor, its endless churning, its confluence between a vast continent and a still vaster ocean evokes more a world of routes than of roots. As a body of water it is Janus-faced, looking backward toward a sea of emigrant crossings—my own people among them— and ahead into a continent forever changed by those endless arrivals. The Narrows is a threshold, physically marked by the enormous bridge that spans it, itself ultimately a gateway to the West and the far coast with its own vast ocean—an Interstate in every sense, one that has some traffic with Hart Crane's ambitious structure: at once retrospect and prospect, and not unlike Thomas McGrath's attempt to span history and the metaphysical in his *Letter to an Imaginary Friend*: "I am a journey toward a distant wound." They present the self as journey, the old story that never leaves but is always new. This poem, *The Narrows*, comprises a mural in verse in which individual poems and sequences link together recursively to form a single dramatic arc, a suspension of movement in time. It begins where I began, in the life given before it is chosen, and ends on the threshold of the one life that is always an afterlife of lives that went before.

"The Narrows"

The epigraph is from Walt Whitman's "Song of Myself." *causey*, Irish usage for causeway; *clachan*, a haphazardly arranged cluster of farmhouses in Irish townlands; *cottier*, a laborer bound to a small parcel of land; *deori*, Irish for "exile;"

meitheall, system of cooperative seasonal famine common in pre-Famine Ireland; *rundale*, pre-Famine system of land distribution in which smaller and smaller parcels of land were made of use to ever larger numbers of Irish peasants; *throughother*, a permission of passage through adjacent fields; *Tir nAn Og*, The Land of Eternal Youth in Irish lore, often associated with America

"The Pier"
The epigraph is from Hart Crane's "Ave Maria" in *The Bridge*. St. John, New Brunswick, was one of the main ports of entry for the famine Irish where, on Partridge Island Quarantine Station, thousands died.

"My Mother at the House of Her Father's Fathers"
boreen, Irish for "small road;" Niobe, Daughter of Tantalus in Greek mythology who wept until she turned to stone after her children were killed by the gods.

"Bay Ridge"
The epigraph is from W.B. Yeats, "Reveries of Childhood and Youth." The lines "at the round earth's imagined corners" in "Prelude: The Narrows," "What if this present were the world's last night" in "Blackout," and the phrase "so richly painted" in "Brown-Eyed Girl" are from John Donne's *Holy Sonnets*.

"A Life Not Lived"
aisling, a vision of Ireland as a beautiful woman; *boke*, Irish slang for puke; *seisun*, a gathering of musicians.

"Pallbearers at Emily Dickinson's Funeral"
The epigraph is from one of Emily Dickinson's poems. *immram*, literally, "voyage" in Irish journey lore, as in *The Voyage of Brendan* or *Mael Dun*.

"At the Lower East Side Tenement Museum"
The epigraph is from Jacob Riis, *How the Other Half Lives*.

"The Island"
The epigraph is from Paul Lawrence Dunbar's poem, "John Boyle O'Reilly."

"Lost Garden Elegies"
The epigraph is from Robert Hayden's poem, "Middle Passage." The first line of the poem alludes to Hayden's "Elegies for Paradise Alley."

"A Mosque in Brooklyn"
The poet is Auden in his poem "Archeology." The last image of the poem alludes to Farid ud-Din Attar's *The Conference of the Birds*.

"At the Tree of Many One"
The title, like the form of this poem, alludes to Wordsworth's "Ode: Intimations of Immortality." The ancient hymn of the fourth section is the Gnostic "Hymn of the Pearl." The poet in the seventh section is Gerard Manley Hopkins. The italicized lines are from *The Cloud of Unknowing*, a 14th Century mystical book written by an anonymous English contemplative.

"Pearl Court"
The epigraph is from Gaston Bachelard's *The Poetics of Space*.

"Back Window"
Drills are rows for planting in Irish usage.

"Thinking of Meade Mountain"
Milerepa is one of the best-loved Tibetan Buddhist saints.

176

"Ballsbridge, Dark Night"
    The form of this poem alludes to Berryman's *The Dream Songs*. Elpenor, friend of Odysseus who, drunk, fell from the roof of Circe's palace and broke his neck.

"Inishboffin Suite"
    Inishboffin Island is off the coast of County Mayo, Ireland. The name means "white cow." Diarmuid and Graine were lovers pursued by Finn McCool in the Fionn Cycle of Irish lore.

"Two Blackouts"
    The epigraph is from Emily Dickinson.

"In the Green-wood"
    The Irish revolutionary Wolfe Tone killed himself in the spirit of the Romans upon his capture during the 1798 Rebellion. After the suicide of her husband, Matilda Tone grudgingly remained in America.

"Twentieth Century Limited"
    The epigraph is from *The Odyssey*, Book 16. The movie alluded to in the beginning of the poem is Wim Wenders' *Wings of Desire*. The writers alluded to are Walt Whitman, Willa Cather, and Hart Crane.

"The Dock Road"
    The last line of the poem is a loose translation of Dante's Inferno, II, lines 141-142, quoted in the epigraph.

"St. John"

The epigraph is from Mary Kilfoil McDevitt's book on St. Mary's, *We Hardly Knew Ye*. The form of the poem alludes to Louis MacNiece's poem, "The Hebrides." The island referred to in the poem is Partridge Island, used as a quarantine station during the influx of famine Irish in the 1840s and 50s. Micmac, Native American tribe indigenous to New Brunswick. Brayon, traditional French Canadian inhabitants of New Brunswick.

"The Ring"

The last lines of this poem are my free translation from the Irish poem "Cois Abha Moire na nDiese," "The Blackwater of the Decies," sung by the late Nioclas Toibin of Rinn na nGael. The Deise names the territory in the southeast of Ireland that later became Waterford and parts of surrounding counties after the British conquest and the re-naming of the land.

"The Rainbow Café"

The doors alluded to in the fifth section of the poem are the Hildescheid Doors in the Busch Reisinger Museum, Harvard University.

"Outerbridge Crossing"

The epigraph is from Czeslaw Milosz's essay, "Migrations." St. Gregory of Nyssa (335-395 CE) was a speculative theologian and mystic of the Capadocian Church. In his theology *apokatatasis*, universal salvation, is the return of all things to God, even, eventually, the damned.

Daniel Tobin is the author of three books of poems, *Where the World is Made*, *Double Life*, and *The Narrows*, a book of criticism, *Passage to the Center: Imagination and the Sacred in the Poetry of Seamus Heaney*, as well as numerous essays on poetry. His poems have appeared widely in such journals as *The Nation*, *The Paris Review*, *Poetry*, *Poetry Ireland Review*, *The Southern Review*, and *The Times Literary Supplement*, and have been anthologized in *Hammer and Blaze*, *The Bread Loaf Anthology of New American Poets*, *The Norton Introduction to Poetry*, and elsewhere. Among his awards are a "Discovery" / *The Nation* Award, the Robert Penn Warren Award, the Robert Frost Fellowship, the Katherine Bakeless Nason Prize, *The Greensboro Review Prize*, and a fellowship from the National Endowment for the Arts. He is Chair of the Department of Writing, Literature, and Publishing at Emerson College in Boston.